Teen Tarot

What the cards reveal about you and your future

Theresa Francis-Cheung and Terry Silvers

Adams Media Corporation
Avon, Massachusetts

In loving memory of our mother, Joyce Margaret Koek.

Published by
Adams Media Corporation
57 Littlefield Street, Avon, MA 02322. U.S.A.
www.adamsmedia.com

ISBN: 1-58062-916-4

Printed in Canada.

J I H G F E D C B A

Library of Congress Cataloging-in-Publication Data
Francis-Cheung, Theresa.
Teen tarot / Theresa Francis-Cheung and Terry Silvers.
p. cm.
Summary: Explains the meaning of different tarot cards and how teenagers can use tarot cards to help solve problems related to family life, school, work, dating, physical health and appearance, and dreams.
ISBN 1-58062-916-4
1. Tarot—Juvenile literature. [1. Tarot.] I. Silvers, Terry. II. Title.
BF1879.T2C52 2003
133.3'2424—dc21
2003001039

Cover and interior illustrations by Roberta Collier Morales

This book is available at quantity discounts for bulk purchases.
For information, cal 1-800-872-5627.

Contents

Acknowledgments

Thank you to all the teens we talked to and worked with when writing this book—your enthusiasm and support were invaluable. Thank you to our Tarot colleagues for their advice and feedback—we couldn't have done it without you. Thank you to Claire Gerus for her wisdom and insight, and for helping us make this book happen. Thank you to Priscilla Stuckey for her fine developmental editing. Thank you to everyone at Adams Media Corporation—especially our editor, Danielle Chiotti, who has been a joy to work with. And, finally, a big thank you for the support of family and friends, especially Ray, Robin, Robert, and Ruth whose love, patience, and support mean the world to us.

Introduction

You picked up this book because you are curious about the Tarot. You've heard all sorts of things about the cards. You may have seen films or television shows in which Tarot card readers appear sinister, and you may worry that either you or someone you know may be getting in too deep by getting involved with the Tarot.

That's okay. It's good to be cautious and caring. If something intrigues you and you are not sure if it is good or bad, you need to find out more so that you can make a rational decision. The Tarot has always held a great deal of mystery throughout the ages, so in these pages we'll separate the facts from the fantasy. You'll learn what the cards can and cannot do. Most important, you'll learn how they can help you make positive changes in your life.

Teen Tarot offers the basics of the Tarot from the point of view of two professional Tarot card readers who aren't too old to remember how tough the teenage years can be. We both started working with the cards in our early teens, and what you'll find in this book has been taken from our years of studying, teaching, and living the Tarot.

A New Doorway

All you need to fully experience this book is curiosity and an open mind. So take a deep breath, grab a hat with wings on, and come along for an amazing journey with lots of surprises along the way.

Enjoy your journey of self-discovery as you read the pages ahead, and remember that the cards are not in the least bit dangerous. Rather, they're an entertaining, informative, and useful guide to your life. It is our great hope that the knowledge you gain from this book will be consistently fascinating and helpful to you.

Consider *Teen Tarot* as your first step into a world of endless possibilities. The book will open a new chapter in your life and give you a different way to think about yourself and the world you live in.

As a trainee Tarot card reader you are entering a new doorway.

May your life never be the same again!

Part One

What Is the Tarot?

✶ The Tarot helps us become conscious—if we desire it.

—Rachel Pollack, *The Open Labyrinth*

1 Making Friends with the Tarot

We are often judged by the company we keep. The friends you hang around with say a lot about the kind of person you are, right? Many people think that your new friend, the Tarot, will corrupt anyone who comes into contact with it. Here are some typical things you may have heard about the cards:

- It's a big con. You can't know what the future holds.
- It's a direct road to hell.
- It can tell you what to do with your life.
- It's a religion.
- You can curse other people with it.

All the above have one thing in common. They are all wrong.

The Tarot can't tell you what to do with your life; only you can do that. There are no Tarot churches, and the Tarot has nothing to do with voodoo or witchcraft. People who say these things about the Tarot don't understand what the cards are really about.

So what are the cards all about? The answer is simple: You.

In the Tarot, you are the star of the show. The cards are like a friend who is fascinated by you. Listening to other people and showing an interest in them is usually the best way to make friends, but the Tarot is a very different kind of friend. The cards will reveal a little about themselves, but mostly the Tarot just keeps asking you questions about yourself. It wants to know everything about you. The Tarot is your number-one fan and your friend for life. You must have had friends that you simply feel you have outgrown—like your first boyfriend or girlfriend, who just makes you cringe when you think about him or her now, or the gang you used to hang around with that you aren't interested in anymore. The wonderful thing about the Tarot is that you never grow out of it. It grows and changes as you grow and change.

You picked this book because you were curious (brilliant start) and because you like to explore out-of-this-world amazing things. It is not like a book at school that you're forced to read. You have made a positive choice to find out more. If you are reading this book for a bit of a joke or because you are bored, the Tarot won't be interested in you as a friend. Stop reading and put it down. Don't get us wrong; the Tarot can be a lot of fun, but to get the best out of it you need to start with serious intentions.

We are assuming that because you are still reading, you want to make friends with the Tarot. Congratulations. With your new best friend at your side, not only will you feel stronger and wiser, you will soon begin to realize that there is nothing ordinary about you or your life anymore. The reason: The Tarot can open your eyes to the opportunity and magic hidden in everything you think, say, and experience.

One last thing before we move on. This book has lots of exercises scattered throughout for you to do. The exercises will help you put into practice what you learn through reading. And what could be more fun than getting to know a new friend?

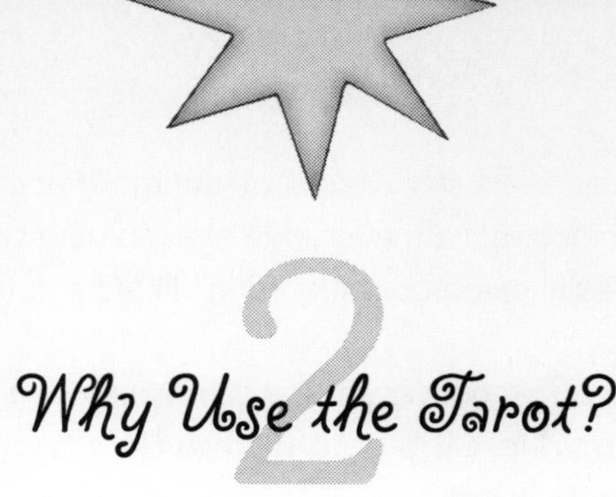

2 Why Use the Tarot?

So why use the Tarot? Because it shows you that you have *choice*.

The Power of Choice

Right now you probably feel as if you have zero control over your life. You don't feel you have many choices about who you are, where you go, what you say, what you do, or what you want. You are not alone. Here are some things a lot of kids told us when we were writing this book:

- "Every adult treats me like a five-year-old. I know I'm young but it doesn't mean I don't have any opinions."
- "I want the freedom to date but my mom doesn't trust men ever since Dad walked out on us."
- "I'm a senior and I should be having fun, but I'm obsessed with getting the best grades I can."
- "I'm sick of having to ask my parents or friends to take me everywhere I want to go. I'm sick of having no money and no way of getting money."
- "I want my parents to hear me out for once instead of telling me 'the answer is no and it's for your own good.'"

- "I've never been very good at anything at school. I'm not going to catch up with everyone else, so who cares?"
- "I don't really care about anything. There's nothing exciting in my life."
- "I'm bored. I've got no plan and have no idea what I want to do with my life. I'll be out there on my own soon and I'm starting to freak out."
- "I go along with my friends not because I want to, but because I'm scared not to."

You probably feel that you don't have the power to make big changes in your life to get what you want. This is where the Tarot cards can help you. They will show you that you do have a lot more choice about the way you live your life than you thought. You just aren't aware of it yet. While it is true that you can't control every aspect of your life, you're not powerless and you're not trapped. You can influence many parts of your life more than you know. You can gain more freedom and more control over what happens to you. You can live with the confidence, self-belief, and enthusiasm that makes you stand out from the crowd. You can live your life in such a way that your parents stop treating you like a kid. You can command the respect of others instead of feeling they are controlling the way you feel. You can set up your life so you stop worrying about it and start living it.

Every situation you face in life gives you a choice. You can let something or someone make you feel and act a certain way, or you can choose to act and feel in the way you think is right. For example, if your boyfriend or girlfriend leaves you, you can let this destroy your confidence, or you can see it as his or her loss. If your grades are poor, you can think that you are useless, or you can decide to do better next time. If you don't feel you have any choice in a situation, self-esteem and confidence plummet. But once you understand that you do have a choice, self-esteem will improve. You aren't a helpless victim anymore. You decide how you deal with a situation. You aren't just reacting to life; you're creating your life.

Using the Tarot will help you become more aware of the consequences of certain decisions you make in life so you can make an informed choice that best suits your interests and those of people around you. In short, the Tarot helps you see that you always have a choice. You choose the way you behave, and if you can't change something, you choose the way you react to it.

Self-Esteem

The Tarot helps you see that you have choice, and with choice come power, confidence, and self-esteem. Self-esteem is a vital ingredient for success and happiness in your life. When you have it you feel good about yourself. You feel calm, confident, and in control, and anything is possible. When you lose it, your confidence and self-belief disappear, and everything starts to go wrong. While we were writing and researching this book, we talked to hundreds of teens about their lives. It seems that every teen is looking for self-esteem, and even the coolest guy or girl suffers from self-doubt. An "A" student with a loving family, a great boyfriend, and a place at college waiting for her said this about herself:

> I feel great one minute and on top of the world, and then something happens or someone says something and the next moment I feel horrible. I feel useless and no good and I don't know what to do to lift myself up again.

A very talented pianist who recently won a scholarship to a prestigious music academy said this about himself:

> I'm really not that gifted. I'm worried that when I get to the academy I will make a mess of things.

It seems that loss of self-esteem is a common experience for teens. Everyone needs to find ways to lift themselves up again when things go wrong. The Tarot answers that need. It can be a great way to build your self-esteem. You'll begin to see that despite all the restrictions put on you, you are not a passenger in your life. You are not a victim or a prisoner. When you start working with the Tarot on a regular basis you'll be astonished at the freedom, power, and choice that you didn't even know you had.

3 Who Uses the Tarot?

Mention the Tarot, and most people think of Gypsies. Although the word *gypsy* is a form of the word *Egyptian*, Gypsies are nomadic people who originally came from India. They did not develop the Tarot, but introduced it to people all over the world, everywhere they traveled.

You probably have an idea in your head of what Gypsies and fortunetellers look like and what they do. You think they're tall, dark-eyed people who live in caravans, wear colorful headscarves, and tell people's fortunes. You are probably also thinking, What a con! Because Gypsies are often very poor, desperation can lead them to give faulty Tarot readings, but it is important to understand that this isn't always the case.

Psychics and mystics also work with the Tarot. They are people who use their intuition and unconscious minds to see things that we don't normally see—like angels or spirits of the dead, or glimpses of the future. They use the Tarot as a way of helping you see what they see. Some psychics tend to give very specific information and tell you what you should or should not do in the future, while others use intuition to glimpse a world of possibility—to see the future as written in sand, not stone. We identify with this latter type, and we hope that by the end of the book, you too will be inspired to use your cards and your intuition to see more possibilities in *your* world.

Many psychologists, psychiatrists, counselors, and therapists also use the Tarot as a way to get information across to clients when other methods fail. In recent years businesses and businesspeople have also started to use the Tarot to help with issues like hiring, firing, and resolving conflicts. When we were teachers we would often use the Tarot to encourage the use of the imagination and develop reading and writing skills in our pupils.

The Tarot can appeal to people from all walks of life, age groups, races, and religions. In more than twenty years of working with the Tarot we have had clients ranging from age six to ninety-six. Every day when you walk down the street you probably pass a Tarot reader but don't realize it. They are unlikely to stand out from the crowd.

Millions of people all over the world use the Tarot, including the rich and famous. Madonna is just one of the many pop stars and celebrities who make regular trips to Tarot readers and psychics. Once Tarot readers were only found at fairgrounds, but now the Tarot has become so totally accepted that you can find them in the shopping mall. Even skeptics are sometimes forced to conclude that there might be something in it.

Downside: The Tarot has become so acceptable that some people are prepared to stake their future on what a Tarot reader tells them. There is a danger if you believe that your future is mapped out already and use the cards as an excuse not to make an effort with your life. For example, if you draw the Nine of Swords one morning you may decide to go back to bed. But this isn't what the Tarot is all about. The Tarot is there to offer you advice—just like teachers, family, and friends do—but at the end of the day you decide whether you listen to it or not. If you can think of the Tarot as a friend offering a point of view, you have exactly the right approach. Remember, the future is never, ever, ever fixed in stone. The Tarot is here to show you that you have the power to create your future by changing your present.

How You Got Here

So you see, all kinds of people use the Tarot to learn about themselves and make better life choices. That's probably why more teens than ever before are turning to the Tarot.

The teenage years can be exciting and difficult. We remember ours as one crisis after another, from high to low and back to high again. It's tough. Everyone seems to tell you what to do, but nobody wants to hear what you have to say. Over and over again you search for the "reason why." Why is this happening to me? Why doesn't anyone understand me? What have I done to deserve this? Why do I have to follow all these rules that don't mean anything to me? If you're like most teens, you could use a way to help you figure out who you are. The cards can do just that. They can help you understand yourself better and be the kind of person you want to be. They can also help you deal with everyday life, the things that happen to you, and the people you meet.

So who uses the Tarot? Curious and interesting people, just like you.

Tarot and Magic

Some people are attracted to the Tarot because they hope to find a little magic. In some ways the Tarot is magical. Magic is defined as the ability to change the circumstances of your life according to your will. The Tarot can certainly help you train and exercise your will. When you read the Tarot cards you understand yourself and the forces that shape you, and this is an essential part of will. How can you change your life without self-knowledge?

An Act of Magic

Many magical acts work through rituals. The ritual helps you raise your energy and will to the point that you feel much more certain about your ability to make positive changes in your life. You don't have to, but if you feel comfortable with this kind of thing, you may want to bring a sense of ritual to your readings. It will help you concentrate. Before you read, light some candles, burn incense, meditate, chant, play music, or do whatever inspires in you a sense of awe. Then when you have laid out your cards, call on your inner guide to help you interpret them. At the end, thank your inner guide and let it go. Blow out your candles, get up and stretch, or turn on the radio—anything to get you back to reality.

The cards give you images and symbols to focus your vague intentions and transform them into action. Your will is the magic. In other words, *you* are the magic. If you can create something in your head and then act on it to make it happen, that is magic. Very simple, very straightforward—no witches, no spells, and no broomsticks. You can get into the more complicated, New Age stuff if you like. Just don't forget that New Age beliefs, like the Tarot, depend on your positive self-growth. They concentrate on making you a better person so that you in turn can help others.

The Tarot is used and respected by people who would probably describe themselves as part of the New Age community. New Age is a term that came into use in the 1960s. It is a relaxed, open-minded way of looking at the world. It's all about trying to be a better and more effective person and using alternative techniques such as the Tarot to help you do this.

There are many thousands of different New Age communities, such as astrologers, numerologists, palmists, and mystics. In Part Two we'll practice a little numerology when we see how to determine which are your soul and personality cards. Many Tarot readers also like to link certain cards to your astrological sign. Look at the following chart. Do you think your star sign and the picture on your assigned card have much in common?

	Date	Element	Card
Aries	March 21–April 20	Fire	The Emperor
Taurus	April 21–May 21	Earth	The Hierophant
Gemini	May 22–June 21	Air	The Lovers
Cancer	June 22–July 23	Water	The Chariot
Leo	July 24–August 23	Fire	Strength
Virgo	August 24–September 23	Earth	The Hermit
Libra	September 24–October 23	Air	Justice
Scorpio	October 24–November 22	Water	Death
Sagittarius	November 23–December 21	Fire	Temperance
Capricorn	December 22–January 20	Earth	The Devil
Aquarius	January 21–February 20	Air	The Star
Pisces	February 21–March 20	Water	The Moon

Many people who consider themselves part of the New Age movement are interested in a wide variety of techniques, like the Tarot, astrology, and numerology. The New Age movement is a bit like going into a clothes shop. You can try on a different "suit" every day in your search for enlightenment. The aim is always the same, though—to search the universe for answers, and to find your own truth.

4 First Steps

The seventy-eight cards of the Tarot have been around for more than 600 years. They have been used for many things, but most of all for divination. Divination is the quest to understand more about the past, present, and future. In other words, Tarot readings are an attempt to understand ourselves better and discover how we might live better in the future.

The Tarot is a book of knowledge and wisdom portrayed in pictures. When you choose a Tarot card, what you will see is a picture of some aspect of yourself or a part of life. Sometimes this will confirm what you already know, but more often than not what you see will intrigue, surprise, annoy, or just amaze you.

Archetype Power

When you think about it, life is a set of pictures or archetypes—ideas or symbols that have been inherited from all sorts of sources. Whether you know it or not, you are interpreting picture symbols all the time. For example, when you see someone smiling at you and another frowning, you are likely to think of the person who is smiling as friendly and the person who is frowning as unfriendly. If you see a red sign, you stop. If you look at the clouds and see gray, it is a pretty safe bet to say it is going to rain..

We all interpret the pictures we see on two levels: personal and universal.

Let's look for a moment at the Five of Pentacles:

This card shows two beggars passing a church. As I look at the card I feel a sense of relief: the beggars have found a place of sanctuary; the church offers protection from the storm.

What I have done here is take an image and project a story onto it. To me this explanation seems obvious—the only possible interpretation of the scene. In fact, someone else could have imagined something totally different. The beggars have not seen the church, or the beggars are too proud to ask for help, or the church has turned away the beggars. After all, the card shows no door to the church.

The point is that of all possible stories I chose a certain one. Why? Because I am projecting my thoughts and feelings onto the picture. We always see the world through the lens of our inner world. This is what makes the Tarot cards so remarkable. Their intriguing pictures and patterns tap into your inner world or unconscious—that part of your mind that you aren't consciously aware of. The Tarot is a mirror that reflects back to you the hidden aspects of yourself. But in addition to the personal meanings you give to a card, each card also has a universal meaning. Let's explain.

As humans we all go through similar emotions and life experiences, and if you look through the Tarot deck you will see a collection of common experiences in a person's lifetime: birth, childhood, work, love, partnership, and death. That's why people often tend to react to the cards in similar ways—because they represent common experiences we all can relate to in some way. Drawing the Death card, for example, is going to create feelings of loss and sadness for most people.

What the Tarot enables you to do is to combine your personal feelings with experiences that are common to all of humankind. You can see each card in your own way, but you can also refer to what others have found meaningful.

Once you start to combine both the personal and the universal, something remarkable happens. You start to see that as powerful as those personal associations and universal experiences are, they are not set in stone. You have the power to change them. For example, if you have always hated cats, holding a little kitten and watching its playful antics may change your personal association. It's the same with universal archetypes. You don't have to accept or agree with them. For example, love isn't just about marriage and 2.4 kids—it can also be about finding your passion in life. Death isn't just about endings; it can also be about new beginnings.

You Are the Force

Every day we are bombarded with nonverbal messages—pictures, images, symbols, and signals from the mirror, your parents, friends, teachers, newspapers, television, and so on. Most people don't realize that they are the ones interpreting these pictures and that the way they interpret them can change their lives.

The fantastic thing about the Tarot is that it can help you see that you are the one who chooses the way you picture your world. It isn't your parents, your teachers, your friends, the mirror, or the media that is the driving force in your life. *You are.* Only when you start to realize that you have the power to choose the way you think, feel, and act can you begin to make positive choices for your future.

5 Where Does the Tarot Come From?

Even though the origins of the Tarot are shrouded in mystery, the important thing to remember is that it comes from a time when people could not read or write. Have you ever been to a church and taken a good long look at the stained glass windows or looked at the illustrations in an old Bible? Hundreds of years ago the priests had to use the pictures rather like a cartoon to explain the Bible stories. Every color, every shape, every detail in a Bible picture means something. The Tarot is like that too. Every card tells a story, and when you take the time to look closely, you will see all sorts of things. For example, green may suggest nature to you, or the position of a foot backward or forward could indicate whether something is a backward or forward step for you.

Our ancestors were far more alive to colors and shapes than we are. They lived as farmers or hunters, and being able to read the landscape around them was vital for their survival. Was a storm coming? Had a herd of animals passed through? What hidden dangers lurked in the woodland? Today we get our food prepared for us at the local supermarket, and with television and personal computers providing so much information, we don't need to picture things in our heads anymore. Our ancestors always had to be aware of personal safety. We do too, but because we're bombarded by so much noise and so many pictures, we aren't always good at observing what is around us.

Although we aren't sure about the origins of the Tarot, it did become very popular in France and Italy during the fourteenth or fifteenth century. Modern-day playing cards are in fact a watered-down version of the original Tarot deck. Certainly many Gypsies wandered around Europe with the cards, and used them to tell fortunes. The majority of medieval people didn't travel, and because Gypsies were always on the go from town to town, buying and selling exotic items as they traveled, Gypsies and the Tarot cards they loved gained a reputation as being exotic and dangerous.

The Tarot really took off in the late nineteenth century. Many Victorians were fascinated by the Tarot, even forming study groups, like the famous Order of the Golden Dawn. One of the members of the London-based Order of the Golden Dawn was a man named Arthur Edward Waite. Waite did not like the existing Tarot packs and decided to design his own.

There are lots of different Tarot card packs out there, but the pack you will see in this book is the Rider-Waite pack. First published in 1910 in London by Rider and Company, the deck was designed by Arthur Edward Waite and an artist named Pamela Coleman Smith. It was based on the dozens of packs that were in circulation at the time. Both Waite and Coleman took a keen interest in medieval history, so you will see that most of the pictures remind you of that time in history. We have used this pack because it is the most popular in the world and the easiest pack for beginners to work with. You can find the Rider-Waite pack very easily in any bookshop or New Age shop that sells Tarot cards. The cards retail at around $10 to $20.

The Tarot really came into its own in the 1960s, when the hippies fell in love with the Tarot. They loved the mystery surrounding the Tarot and adored its unconventional way of explaining the world. After several rock bands included Tarot cards on their album covers, the cards became a fashion statement for the love-and-peace generation, along with a flower in the hair. This explosion of interest resulted in a large number of new Tarot packs, and many of the packs you see in shops today have modern designs. Their creators, however, would argue that the new designs are based on principles that go back to the dawn of time.

As we enter the new millennium, things haven't changed very much for the Tarot. The cards are used in much the same way as they were centuries ago. A traditional Tarot reading involves a seeker, who has questions to ask, and a reader, who knows how to interpret the cards. After the seeker has shuffled and cut the pack, the reader lays out the chosen cards in a pattern called a spread. Each position in the spread has a meaning, and each card has a meaning as well. The reader combines these two meanings to shed light on the seeker's question.

It's a simple process, but it's rarely presented in a straightforward way. In films we still see stereotypical Tarot readings taking place in a seedy parlor or back room. An old woman seated in shadows reads the cards for a nervous young girl. The crone lifts her wrinkled finger and drops it ominously on the Death card. The girl faints with fear.

This aura of fear and darkness still clings to the Tarot cards today. Some religions shun the cards, and many experts condemn them as symbols of unreason, but, as pointed out earlier, these judgments are based on ignorance about what the cards actually can and cannot do. The cards are not foolish or evil or dangerous in the slightest if used in the right way.

Fortunately, things are changing as more and more people (like you) learn how to use the cards properly and with respect and find that they receive great wisdom in return. So from now on, let's set aside these false, shadowy images of the Tarot and think about what it actually is—a pack of picture cards with the power to change your life for the better, if used correctly. The first question we should be asking is, Where do they get their power?

6 Where Do the Cards Get Their Power?

The Tarot gets its power from you. Let's explain.

The answer lies within your unconscious mind—that part of your mind that operates outside your everyday experience. It is a world of hunches, insight, intuition, and ideas you have inherited from a variety of sources; it's a world of dreams and knowing things without really being sure why. We all have within us a wisdom and power we simply aren't tapping into.

Your unconscious mind is in many ways like a computer. An incredible amount of data is filed in its memory banks—more than can ever be stored in your conscious mind. Everything you ever saw, heard, felt, tasted, and smelled is there. We may never know the full range and power of the unconscious mind. Not a single one of you reading this book is living up to your own possibilities. It is estimated that even the brightest of people use just a tiny percentage of their brain capacity.

Ever had this experience? You are struggling to recall someone's name and "it's right on the tip of my tongue" but you give up trying. Later, seemingly out of nowhere, when you are thinking of something else, the answer pops unexpectedly into your mind. That's a typical example of your unconscious mind at work. By consciously trying to find this bit of information and then forgetting about it, you triggered a search through all the memory banks of your unconscious mind while you engaged in other activities.

Your subconscious mind is a storehouse of information and is far more complicated and powerful than any computer. It sees and knows what your conscious mind misses. Whereas your conscious mind can only handle one thought at a time, your unconscious mind can comprehend, store, and remember millions of bits of data every second. It never sleeps; it functions unceasingly even when you are asleep or thinking about other things. Many techniques, such as meditation, dream interpretation, visualization, and psychotherapy, try to explore the unconscious. The Tarot is another such tool. The cards have no power of their own. They are a tool or guide for you to get in touch with your own inner power.

The Tarot is simply one of the best tools available for you to seek inspiration and guidance from your unconscious. The ideas, images, and feelings that emerge as you work are messages from your unconscious. When you reach for the Tarot pack, you signal to your unconscious (you may like to call it your inner guide or your angel) that you are ready for wisdom.

We are meant to rely on the wisdom of our inner guide, but somehow we have forgotten to access it. We trust our conscious minds instead and forget to look deep inside ourselves. Our conscious minds are clever, but unfortunately they don't have the full awareness we need to make appropriate choices every day. When you operate from your conscious mind you may feel as if life is happening to you and you haven't got a purpose. Until you become aware of *what* you have been conditioned to think, you will go through life without consciously realizing *why* you think, say, and do certain things. Basically, you feel out of control. However, when you use the Tarot to make contact with your inner wisdom, you experience life differently. You discover your inner potential and the power of positive choice.

The Meaning of the Tarot

When you do a Tarot reading you select certain cards by shuffling, cutting, and dealing the deck. The process is random. Now, common sense tells us that cards chosen at random can't be special—or can they?

To answer this, let's look at randomness more closely. When we say an event is random, we mean it is the result of chance events. However, no Tarot reading is caused purely by chance. You made the conscious decision to study the Tarot cards and choose a card. At every step you are actively involved. We know our card choices aren't deliberate, so we call them random. But we cannot ignore the possibility that our unconscious is directing our choice of cards.

The other characteristic of a random event is that it has no meaning. But perhaps there is purpose and meaning to every event, however small, and we just don't recognize it. Tarot readers believe that there is a message in everything—trees, songs, even trash—but only when we are open to receiving it. The Tarot cards can only communicate meaning if you have a sincere wish to find out about yourself and improve your life.

Fun Exercise

There are thousands of different Tarot card packs out there, each with a different design. Now, we'd like you to look through the illustrations in this book and have a go at redesigning any card that strikes your fancy. You can redesign it on paper or in your mind's eye. For example, you might want to redraw the Wheel of Fortune as one of the big Las Vegas casinos, or imagine the Emperor as the president. Who knows, in years to come you may go on to redesign all seventy-eight cards and get them printed around the world!

7
Let's Go Shopping

According to tradition, you should never buy a Tarot pack; you should wait until somebody else is guided by the stars and heavens to give you one. Chances are if you do that, you will be waiting a long time! What this really means is that you can't buy the wisdom the cards have; you can only learn it. You don't really have to wait for someone to give you a pack. Either ask someone to give you a pack as a present, or save some money and buy one for yourself.

There are many other Tarot packs out there. Here are just some of the many you could choose from:

- The Nordic Tarot: pictures from Viking legends.
- The Greek Tarot: pictures of ancient Greek gods.
- The Spiral Tarot: pictures from Celtic mythology.
- The African Tarot: African-American symbols.
- The Renaissance Tarot: Renaissance art depicting Roman and Greek gods.
- The Santa Fe Tarot: Navajo Native American theme.
- The Native American Tarot: Native American art from across the United States.
- The Mother Peace Tarot: women-centered drawings.

We could go on and on. Whatever your taste, there is a Tarot deck for you. If you are buying a pack to frighten others and are deliberately looking for a pack that looks horrific, stop reading this book now! It is always important in life to do something because you want to do it, not because you want to look big in front of others.

You may want to find a pack from a background that suits you or that you are sympathetic to. For example, if you have an African-American background you will understand the African Tarot pack far better than someone who is not African-American. The only limitation with the Rider-Waite pack is that it lacks ethnic diversity, and if you are not Caucasian you may not as easily see aspects of yourself in the cards. Do bear in mind that the messages the cards give have universal meaning; race and culture don't really enter into it. The important thing, though, is that you feel comfortable with your cards. If you want a pack that reflects your background, by all means get one.

If you enjoy looking at catalogs, the most comprehensive is published by U.S. Games Systems, Inc. You can order one by calling 1-800-544-2637 or writing to U.S. Games Systems, Inc., 179 Ludlow Street, Stamford, CT 06902. If you love surfing the Net, you can check out *www.usgamesinc.com* or enter "Tarot decks" in your search engines.

Tarot decks come in all shapes, sizes, and designs. Some people collect packs like stamps or trading cards. Choose a pack that feels right in your hands and is easy to shuffle. If you have or want to buy a pack that isn't Rider-Waite, you can still use this book, because the names and numbers of the cards are the same, but we do suggest you stick with the Rider-Waite and leave the other packs until you have familiarized yourself with this one first. If you really want another unusual pack, it might be a good idea to buy two packs. One would be the pack that you really like, which you can move on to later when you have finished learning with the Rider-Waite. After all, you don't go straight to Shakespeare to learn to read!

Getting to Know Your Cards

Everyone learns best by doing rather than listening, so if you have a pack of cards already, let's get started.

Sort out the pack into five piles. The first pile will be the twenty-two Major Arcana cards. These are numbered 0 to 21, beginning with The Fool and ending with The World. In some packs these cards are not numbered and are simply known by their names, such as The Lovers, The Chariot, The Sun, and so on. The second pile will be all of the cards with Cups on them. You'll find fourteen of them—1 through 10, Page, Knight, King, and Queen of Cups. The third pile will be Swords, the fourth will be Pentacles, and the fifth will be Wands. All three of these suits are numbered the same as the Cups.

Now shuffle each pile and choose one card from each pile at random. Lay the cards in front of you, so you have one Major Arcana card, one card from the suit of Cups, one from the Swords, one from the Pentacles, and one from the Wands. As you do this, think about what you would like to learn from the Tarot cards. If you don't have your pack yet, take a look at Part Two and choose a card from each section. Don't look at the meanings of the cards at this point. Write down which cards you choose, and after studying the pictures for a few moments write down what each picture makes you think and feel.

My Major Arcana card is______________________________.

This card makes me feel or think of________________________.

My Cups card is____________________________________.

This card makes me feel or think of________________________.

My Swords card is__________________________________.

This card makes me feel or think of________________________.

My Pentacles card is ______________________________.

This card makes me feel or think of________________________.

My Wands card is ________________________________.

This card makes me feel or think of________________________.

As you work on this exercise, remember that the Tarot is not like a lesson at school. There is no wrong or right answer. If The Lovers card makes you feel sad, instead of happy as you think you ought to, write it down. If you feel something genuinely, it is right!

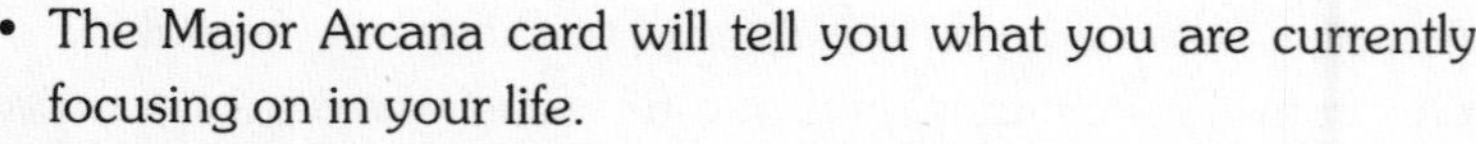

- The Major Arcana card will tell you what you are currently focusing on in your life.
- The Cups card will tell you what you feel about yourself.
- The Swords card will tell you what challenges or upsets you.
- The Pentacles card will tell you what your attitude is toward money.
- The Wands card will tell you what you need to work on in your life.

Don't worry if you can't quite make sense of anything you have written down. We can assure you it will make sense eventually. At the end of the book we will ask you to have a look at this exercise again. You will then see how far you have moved on from your first impressions. For now, just look through the cards, the colors, the landscapes, the people, the animals, and so on in as much detail as possible, and think about how individual cards make you feel.

Part Two

Pick a Card, Any Card: Introducing the Tarot Deck

✶ There is no sense of getting it wrong, really; only of weaving the symbolism which the Tarot has to offer into the context of your own life.

—Terry Donaldson, *Step by Step Tarot*

8 Secrets That Aren't Secrets Anymore:

The Twenty-Two Cards of the Major Arcana

Part Two will serve as a reference tool to help you get to know your Tarot deck. We'll begin with the twenty-two cards of the Major Arcana. Read the information about the Major and Minor Arcana, and dip in and out of the rest. You'll find that we constantly refer back to the cards and their meanings in the rest of the book.

Don't forget, there are an infinite number of meanings for each card. This little book can't cover them all. If you feel that there is more to a card than we have outlined here, you are probably right.

What Does Arcana Mean?

The word *arcana* has its roots in the Latin word *arcanum*, meaning secret, and the French word *arca* meaning chest, box, or container. Both *arca* and *arcanum* mean the mystery of mysteries, or ultimate secrets or mysterious knowledge known only to a few. In other words, *arcana* literally means a box of secrets, and the Tarot deck contains important secrets about who you are and how the world works. Think of the Major and Minor Arcana as a box of human wisdom and experience.

Earlier we discussed archetypes and how there are two of them: personal ones, which are based on your personal experiences, and universal ones, which are based on the experiences of humanity. You need to consider both the personal and the universal as you read the cards, and remember that the power of the Tarot comes from your awareness of archetypes, both personal and universal. It is only when you become aware of and start to change your archetypes (or the way you see things) that you start to change yourself.

As we go through life we often think of ourselves in terms of archetypes. How many times have you squirmed when adults described you as a "typical teen"? How many times have you classed people into a certain group: the old granny, the doting mother, the strict teacher, and so on? I'm sure if you really got to know these people, you might be surprised by what you found out. Perhaps the "old lady" writes crime novels in her spare time, the "doting mother" is struggling to come to terms with her role in life, and the "strict teacher" spends his weekends helping disabled children. Just as there is nothing typical about you, there is always a great deal more to every person than meets the eye. Remember, archetypes are not fixed in stone. You can always challenge, question, change, and re-create them, and as you do this you challenge, question, change, and re-create your life.

The Major Arcana

The cards in the Major Arcana are called "major" because they deal with the big issues in life. The twenty-two cards all contain pictures or archetypes of major emotional states in life that most of us will experience at one time or another.

The Major Arcana cards are about the journey you will take through childhood into adult life, and they pinpoint typical problems and the opportunities you will face. Think about the journey of your life so far. You probably already have experienced changes of direction and pace. Your family might have moved several times. Middle school will certainly be different from high school. Your friends today are probably not the friends you had five years ago. You are changing all the time, going through different emotional states and trying out different archetypes. In short, your life is a journey, and you should think of the Major Arcana as a map or guide you can use to point you in the right direction.

It's a Girl and Guy Thing

As you look through the cards you'll notices lots of references to "he" or "she." Some of the cards have men on them; some of them have women on them. The Rider-Waite Tarot deck was produced in 1920, when gender stereotyping was still strong, but thankfully, equality of the sexes is making that a thing of the past. So if you are a girl and you get a card with lots of masculine references, or a boy who gets a card with lots of feminine references, what the cards are trying to tell you is that you need to develop the qualities associated with the card. For example, if you are a girl, a masculine card may recommend that you take a few more risks. If you are a boy, a feminine card may suggest that you be more considerate. The development of qualities traditionally associated with the opposite sex will help you become a more complete person.

Getting Ready

Generally the first seven cards of the Major Arcana suggest what you need to do to achieve success in the world. The Tarot is not a religion, but it does try to help you become a better person. That is what cards 8 to 14 focus on. Cards 15 to 22 are about going back into the outer world and putting into practice all the lessons you have learned.

For each card we give some general information, and then we

relate the card to various aspects of your life that may concern you at the present: friends, school, dating, family, interests, health/looks, and money. You'll see that we talk about symbols a lot. Symbols are simply things that represent something else. For example, a cross represents religion for many people. A chocolate bar is a sign of comfort. We also add a caution or downside with each card. Don't worry too much about those. Later in the book we'll discuss negative meanings and reversals in more detail, but for now, just bear in mind that no card is totally good or totally bad. Within each negative experience there is the potential for positive, and within each positive experience there is the potential for negative. We've seen that how you read life determines what life means to you, and since life is always a combination of positive and negative, the cards should be interpreted that way, too. Finally, you'll notice a thirty-second reading for each card. This is our way of getting to the core of a card's meaning by relating it to a real-life example. Keep in mind that this thirty-second reading is only one of 100—or 1,000—ways that the card might relate to real life.

And now, if you are ready, let's journey through the past, present, and future of your life. Let's explore the Major Arcana.

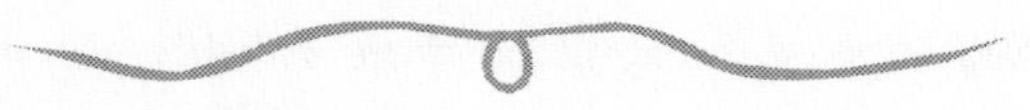

0: THE FOOL

The Fool, or Joker, is about to step off a cliff into the unknown—the unknown represents an uncertain future—but he is clearly not worried about anything. Never underestimate the Fool. He may seem carefree and foolish, but he can also be insightful. We all know that there is truth in jokes. Have you ever noticed your teacher smile when she or he makes a sarcastic comment, like "good afternoon" when you arrive late for morning class? The intention is to make a point but to do it in a humorous way rather than a hurtful one. If The Fool appears in a reading, he is trying to convey something to you in a lighthearted way. The hope is that you will get the point and won't need to find out the hard way. What The Fool wants you to know is that it is time to start laying the foundations for the rest of your life. This doesn't mean you should stop having fun, it just means that it isn't good enough anymore to react to what life throws at you and make things up as you go along. It is time to start thinking about what you want in life.

Questions to ask yourself if you draw The Fool:

- Are you about to start something new, a relationship, a class?
- Do you know what makes you happy?
- Is it time for you to do what you feel you must and not what others expect you to do?
- Are you ready for change?
- Should you pay more attention to your heart and less to your head?
- Have you been a little foolish lately? Is it time for some serious thinking?

Friends

UPSIDE: New friends are coming into your life. They will have lots of new ideas, and you can look forward to an exciting social life.

DOWNSIDE: New friends, but you should be wary of them. Spending time with them will have a negative effect on you because they haven't got your best interests at heart.

KEY THOUGHTS:

Learn to distinguish between being foolish and being a fool. It is not uncool to work hard for the things that you want. It is not uncool to get excited about something in life, to find a passion.

School

UPSIDE: You will be putting an effort into some new subjects that turn out to be a lot more interesting than you thought.

DOWNSIDE: You tend to lose interest in most projects despite promising yourself and your teachers that you will make the effort this time. Try to finish at least one of your tasks this week. It will be worth your while.

Dating

UPSIDE: The start of a new romance. You have met, or will meet, an exciting, fun-loving companion who will be important in your life for many years to come.

DOWNSIDE: You will have the opportunity to get close to someone you think is exciting but who is really selfish and irresponsible. Avoid that person. You don't need him or her in your life.

Family

UPSIDE: Lots of changes to your family circumstances. These changes open up new opportunities for you to get close to one member of your family in particular.

DOWNSIDE: Think about the consequences of your actions. If you want excitement, get a new interest. Don't try to find it by upsetting those who love you the most.

Interests

UPSIDE: An unusual new hobby or interest is coming your way. This is probably the start of a lifelong interest.

DOWNSIDE: Take care with any out-of-the-ordinary interruptions to your routine. They might give you short-term pleasure, but they will cause you a lot of problems in the long run.

Health/Looks

UPSIDE: You feel good about the way you look and aren't really bothered about what other people think. Congratulate yourself!

DOWNSIDE: Are you spending too much time in front of the mirror? There is a difference between feeling good about the way you look and vanity.

Money

UPSIDE: Money is a worry for you, but you aren't letting lack of funds get you down. You find ways to have fun without getting into debt.

DOWNSIDE: You have been careless with money recently. Try putting a little money aside each week instead of spending it on things you don't really need.

30-SECOND READING

Melissa was in a state. She was halfway through a history assignment and had lost her notes. She was overcommitted to a range of extracurricular activities, like judo and cheerleading, and was constantly letting everybody down. The Fool came up. Her best approach now was to be honest and tell people she was in a muddle. She needed to inform all the teachers and groups that she needed time to sort herself out and work out what she could and could not commit to. The Fool can be a bit aimless and directionless at times, and when it appears in a reading it suggests a need for structure, discipline, wise choices, and organization.

1: THE MAGICIAN

Like The Fool before him, The Magician signifies new beginnings. Notice the vibrancy of the colors. The Magician wears red, which is the color of action. The bright yellow background suggests the dawning of a new day. The natural scenes, along with the colors red and yellow, all symbolize the hope and excitement of something new. Unlike The Fool, though, more thought has been put into the direction the new beginning will take. The creativity isn't careless; it is focused. There is a great sense of purpose about this card. The Magician has the ability to translate ideas into action. He has a strong will and a lot of self-confidence, and uses these qualities to direct his life where he wants to go. Congratulations—whether you know it or not, you are moving into the driver's seat of life. You are setting the wheels in motion, which is often the hardest part.

Questions to ask yourself if you draw The Magician:

- Is there an area of your life you need to make changes in?
- Are you a jack-of-all-trades but master of none?
- Is there a need for more creativity in your life?
- Are you dreaming rather than doing?
- Are you resisting change?

Friends

UPSIDE: People are drawn to you because there is a kind of magic about you. You are fun to hang around with and have remarkable powers of communication.

DOWNSIDE: Laziness is stopping you from getting to know new people and experiencing new things. Make a fresh start today. Stop watching life; start living it.

School

UPSIDE: A good time to make choices about assignments or subjects where you want to concentrate your energies. These choices will help you decide on your future career. It is not uncool to want a better life and work toward getting it.

DOWNSIDE: You are delaying making decisions about schoolwork or simply not putting the effort in it. If action isn't taken soon you will regret it. Life isn't a dress rehearsal. This is the real thing. Make the effort, and you will feel so much better about yourself.

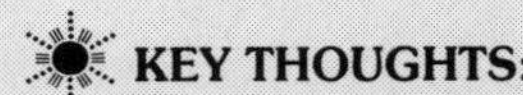

There are opportunities all around you to alter the course of your life. Stop waiting for them to come to you. Go out and find them. The future isn't written in the stars. You can create your own experience and become the star of your own life.

Dating

UPSIDE: You have enough confidence to initiate a new romance. The other person will be more than willing to follow your lead. Go on, ask him or her out!

DOWNSIDE: You tend to give up too easily and often sit on the sidelines watching everyone else have more fun. You have a lot to offer but must work on your own self-confidence. If you don't like yourself, why should anyone else like you?

Family

UPSIDE: Your family is noticing that you are behaving more and more like an adult. This is because you are discussing things with them, paying attention to their feedback, and directing your energy positively.

DOWNSIDE: Try to show more respect to those around you. Your attitude is causing unnecessary tension.

Interests

UPSIDE: You are starting to notice the magic in everyday life. Now is the time for setting clear goals. They will pay off, so think big!
DOWNSIDE: You are finding life a little tedious at the moment. You may be wasting too much time on unimportant leisure pursuits like television or computer games. Life is for living; don't let it pass you by. Talk to your friends and family instead of hiding in your room.

Health/Looks

UPSIDE: You are about to totally revamp your image. Have fun with it!
DOWNSIDE: Your personal style could do with some improvement. Something isn't working. Perhaps you could benefit from regular exercise, a healthier diet, or just a more positive attitude.

Money

UPSIDE: It is possible that money will be coming your way shortly or you will be offered a means to make that money, with a part-time job or extra chores at home. Take that opportunity.
DOWNSIDE: Don't spend money when you feel distracted or restless. That isn't the answer. Direct your energies to a creative pursuit, or talk to your family, friends, or teachers about starting a new class or hobby.

30-SECOND READING

The Magician often represents a powerful male influence. Dean was having a lot of problems with his father. His father wasn't visiting him much since his parents had divorced. Dean felt very hurt every time his father canceled a meeting or turned up hours late. Dean didn't respect his dad and thought he was a liar. The Magician in Dean's spread indicates that Dean is right to be

(continued)

concerned about his father, who isn't the responsible, stable figure Dean needs right now. But the card suggests that it is up to Dean's dad, and not Dean, to make the effort right now. Dean needs to stop getting angry with his dad (it won't achieve anything), get on with his life, and seek out other positive male role models in his school or family.

2: THE HIGH PRIESTESS

The High Priestess is a mysterious figure who sits between a dark pillar and a light pillar. She symbolizes neutrality between the positive and the negative. There is a veil attached to the temple entrance, which represents the mystery of life. We can't see or go beyond the veil yet because we don't have the skills needed to fully understand what lies behind it. At the moment all we can do is look, learn, and wonder. The card often suggests intuitive or psychic gifts and the need to learn from those around you. It also indicates a need for peace and calm. Sometimes just being still is a good idea, because it gives you a chance to reflect on your life and why you do the things you do. Many of us avoid change by avoiding problems or shortcomings. The High Priestess warns against this.

Questions to ask yourself if you draw The High Priestess:

- What is your intuition telling you?
- Who in the world would you like to be, and what qualities do you admire most in that person? How can you acquire these qualities for yourself?

- Are you being true to yourself?
- Would you benefit from some thinking time?
- Are you getting too involved with other people and forgetting who you are?
- What are your dreams trying to tell you?

Friends

UPSIDE: People are lucky to have you as a friend because you listen carefully to their problems without judging. You have the ability to mix with all types of people. This card could also mean you have a gentle, caring friend who is doing a lot to help you.

DOWNSIDE: You are being swept along by peer pressure and are not thinking for yourself. This could get you into lots of trouble. Many of your so-called friends will be happy to let you take the rap for problems they started.

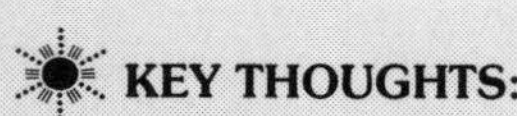

KEY THOUGHTS:

Don't follow the group; instead, do what your heart tells you to do. You cannot change what you do not acknowledge. Get real about what is bothering you. This is the time to make personal decisions and accept responsibility for them.

School

UPSIDE: You know what is required to do well at school. Keep trusting your instincts about what is right or wrong, and don't be influenced by the chatter of some of your friends.

DOWNSIDE: Stop going with the crowd, and start thinking for yourself.

Dating

UPSIDE: The kind of relationship that you need right now is one in which both people are attentive to the other's needs. If you are in a relationship with someone, you need to feel that he or she is your soul mate. If there is any doubt in your mind, don't commit yourself to something you may regret.

DOWNSIDE: You are neglecting other areas in your life and wasting too much time waiting for someone to call. Develop other interests. Let other people fall in love with you not because you are looking for love, but because you love many things in your life.

Family

UPSIDE: You are handling family problems well and showing an understanding beyond your years. Pat yourself on the back.
DOWNSIDE: You are getting overinvolved in your family's problems. Don't let their problems overshadow your own very real needs.

Interests

UPSIDE: You have had a number of psychic experiences in your life and are investigating and building on this skill.
DOWNSIDE: Telling people you are a psychic is not a way to find your identity. Find out who you are first, and then think about developing your psychic powers.

Health/Looks

UPSIDE: There is always something out-of-this-world about you. This mysterious quality suits you and intrigues other people.
DOWNSIDE: Don't get so involved with psychic matters that you neglect your health. Keep eating well, stop losing or gaining weight, and get lots of fresh air and exercise.

Money

UPSIDE: Money isn't that important to you. You can take it or leave it. This gives you a sense of freedom and opens the doors to creativity.
DOWNSIDE: Just because you don't need money to feel happy, don't neglect the importance of money either. Watch the pennies and save whenever you can. Used wisely, money can do untold good both for yourself and others.

30-SECOND READING

Latoya has strange dreams and insights about the future. She always knows who is on the phone when it rings. She has tried talking to her mother about this, but her mother thinks Latoya is making it all up. The High Priestess often indicates the influence of a woman in someone's life. For Latoya it confirms that she is psychic; however, it is also the card of secrets. It is telling her that she should keep this part of her life secret until she is a little older. Then she will be able to investigate it on her own terms and perhaps someday have an intelligent conversation about it with her mother.

3. THE EMPRESS

The card shows a woman sitting in lush surroundings. She is surrounded by fertility symbols, which is why this card is often connected with creativity and pregnancy. The Empress is longing to bring her children, symbolizing her passions, into the world. She represents the kind of love, like mother love, that is given without thought, conditions, or judgment. Sometimes, thinking too deeply about something you care about can spoil it. Have you ever concentrated on something so hard at school that you stopped enjoying it? The Empress says stop analyzing, go with the flow, and enjoy being creative. Television, computer games, and Net surfing are often the enemies of creativity because all the work is done for you. The Empress is about using your talents wisely. It suggests a time of growth and opportunity, a good period for relationships and money. It is also about creating your own life. If you don't like the way people are treating you, change the way you react to them.

Questions to ask yourself if you draw The Empress:

- What do you want to create?
- Who are the female role models in your life?
- Are you creating good or bad experiences in your life?
- What is your heart's desire?
- Is anything blocking your creativity?
- What or who are you mothering?

Friends

UPSIDE: You are very supportive of your friends. They come to you for advice, and you give it. This card could also indicate your need for advice and guidance.

DOWNSIDE: You are spending too much time alone or sitting in your room listening to music and playing computer games. Think about why you are doing this. If you fear rejection, remember that everyone, even the most confident, fears rejection. You can't let fear rule your life; if you do, you will end up with no life at all.

School

UPSIDE: This is a good time to get involved with creative subjects like music, drama, and art. They will provide you with a great deal of pleasure.

DOWNSIDE: You are in danger of burning out because you are doing too much. Take it easy.

Dating

UPSIDE: If you want to meet someone new, go out and experience new things. You never know who you might meet along the way.

DOWNSIDE: Don't even think about getting pregnant, or getting someone pregnant, in order to move your relationship forward. At such a young age, this is not the best way to move things along.

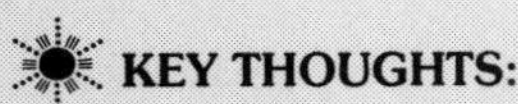

KEY THOUGHTS: Use your resources wisely and in a balanced way. You are responsible for your life. Don't be someone you are not. Create the experiences you want out of life, and teach other people how to treat you.

Family

UPSIDE: There is a mother figure or a woman filled with passion and integrity who brings beauty, harmony, and love to your life.

DOWNSIDE: There could be an overpowering female figure in your life, or a smothering love that makes you feel suffocated.

Interests

UPSIDE: Gardening, outdoor pursuits, or a new creative project involving nature will be very important over the next couple of months.

DOWNSIDE: Stop thinking that you can't be creative. If you tell other people you are boring, they will believe you. Everyone can be creative. It just takes a little courage and self-belief. Think better of yourself.

Health/Looks

UPSIDE: You have the radiant glow of health and vitality about you.

DOWNSIDE: Are you making enough of an effort with your appearance? Just a little more effort, and you'll be amazed by how much better you feel and look.

Money

UPSIDE: Some of your moneymaking ideas have potential. Think about ways you can translate your ideas into financial reward.

DOWNSIDE: Don't let greed stand in the way of your heart's desire. If you don't feel happy or fulfilled, it doesn't matter how much money you have.

30-SECOND READING

Hassana wants to leave college and get a job, but is sure her family will want her to continue with her studies. She does not know what to do. The Empress tells her that if she is really serious about getting a good job, continuing her studies is important. The Empress is a positive card, and it reassures her that although the path ahead won't be easy, she will eventually get her life back on track.

4: THE EMPEROR

The Emperor signifies masculinity, order, and discipline. You will notice that the Emperor holds a globe in his left hand, which shows that he is concerned more with the outside world than the inner world. His focus is very much on providing discipline for a chaotic world in need of rules. The solidly built throne he sits on symbolizes his immense power. Structure is necessary to make sure that the creativity of The Emperor bears fruit. People often say that success is 5 percent inspiration and 95 percent hard work. Taken too far, however, discipline can stifle creativity and result in routine for the sake of routine. Look at how severe and bad-tempered this man looks. Has he concentrated so much on outward achievement that he has forgotten to listen to what his heart is telling him?

Questions to ask yourself if you draw The Emperor:

- What is your relationship with your father or authority figures like?
- Is something overpowering you?
- Is there a need for rules, organization, and regulation in your life?
- Would you benefit from assertiveness training?
- Do you need to be more reasonable?
- Do you need better male role models?

Friends

UPSIDE: You are showing excellent leadership skills with your friends at the moment. Your friends take your lead, so make sure you lead them wisely.

DOWNSIDE: You are dominating your friends at the moment, or being dominated by them. Stop being heavy-handed, or steer clear of heavy-handed people.

School

UPSIDE: You are working well with your teachers. One particular male teacher is proving to be an excellent role model to you at the moment.

DOWNSIDE: You are in conflict with your teachers. Stop thinking that they are picking on you, and remember why you are at school: to learn, and learning involves self-improvement.

Dating

UPSIDE: You may be drawn to someone who is a little older and wiser than you.

DOWNSIDE: Don't drown yourself in a relationship. Sooner or later you are going to need the outside world. Don't get so wrapped up that the outside world forgets about you.

Family

UPSIDE: You have good role models who are providing you with sensible rules for living your life. It is good to see you following these rules without supervision.

DOWNSIDE: You feel stifled by the rules and regulations in your life. Make sure you talk to your parents or teachers about your need for greater autonomy.

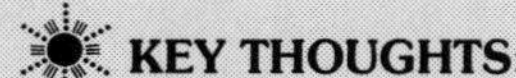

KEY THOUGHTS:

Face your problems, don't ignore them. Don't accept a crummy situation, but instead see what you can do to change it.

Interests

UPSIDE: Debating and leadership positions on committees or groups are at center stage in your life, or will be soon.

DOWNSIDE: Stop criticizing and disrupting from the sidelines. Get involved.

Health/Looks

UPSIDE: You take care with your appearance and are always dressed appropriately, whatever the occasion.

DOWNSIDE: Your disciplined approach to your body is starting to make you feel unwell. Relax a little, and take some time off from your regime.

Money

UPSIDE: You are the kind of person who is able to make the best use of your money. Congratulate yourself. This is an invaluable skill to have later in life.

DOWNSIDE: Rebelling by getting into debt isn't going to achieve anything. It is going to make you poor, your parents unhappy, and your friends uncomfortable.

30-SECOND READING

John really wants to go to college, and needs to start earning credits for his high school diploma. Matters came to a head when he got a D on a history essay. The Emperor card indicates that it is all up to John. He can achieve his dreams and get to college if he works a little harder. The Emperor is the card of iron self-discipline. He needs to show that quality now.

5: THE HIEROPHANT

This card signifies the importance of spirituality and tradition. Like the Emperor, the Hierophant, or Pope, can be a little too concerned with rules and regulations, and this can make him look severe and unhappy. Two monks are bowing to him. These monks represent the desire in all of us for answers to the big questions of life, such as why we are here. The pillars on either side of the Hierophant are gray—not black or white—which means that you won't make a lot of progress if you let other people direct your life for you or answer your questions for you. By all means listen to what The Hierophant has to say, but then use what you have learned to find the truth within your own heart.

Questions to ask yourself if you draw The Hierophant:

- Is religion turning you on or off?
- Are you in need of advice or guidance?
- Are you rebelling against authority?

- Do you understand that the best teacher is within you?
- Do you listen, really listen, to what other people have to say?
- Do you realize that you are the one who finally decides what is right or wrong?

Friends

UPSIDE: You are a reliable, compassionate, loyal, and trustworthy friend.

DOWNSIDE: You are too easily led at the moment. Try thinking for yourself a bit more.

School

UPSIDE: You are finding that your teachers are a source of inspiration and guidance. Their approval means a lot to you.

DOWNSIDE: You are in conflict with teachers, but this really disguises the fact that you don't understand the work. Next time you are tempted to act up in class, ask for help and be surprised by the amount of advice, support, and encouragement you receive.

Dating

UPSIDE: Your interest in religion or spirituality will lead to new friendships. One of these could lead, or has already led, to romance.

DOWNSIDE: You are being cynical and seeing only the negative in people. Stop it. Take time to get to know people before you pass judgment.

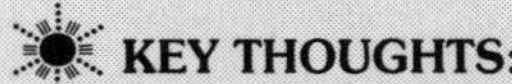

The problem-free, stress-free life doesn't exist. The secret isn't to avoid setbacks but to learn how to manage them well.

Family

UPSIDE: You have received and acted on some wise counsel from a parent or a parent figure.

DOWNSIDE: Listen before interrupting when family members speak. Stop trying to be the center of attention all the time, and put yourself in someone else's shoes.

Interests

UPSIDE: You have started to get interested in religion and spirituality. The insight and knowledge you gain will lead to new confidence.
DOWNSIDE: Avoid all kinds of superstition or fanatical religion.

Health/Looks

UPSIDE: There is someone in your life or the media whom you admire. Let them inspire you to create your own personal style. You will be pleased with the results.
DOWNSIDE: Your need for outside approval about your appearance isn't helping you feel good about yourself. Much of the advice you are getting isn't helping you. Trust your instincts, and cultivate a look that you, and not somebody else, feel good about.

Money

UPSIDE: You already have or could soon team up with a friend or family member for a moneymaking venture. You can trust this person. It will be a success.
DOWNSIDE: You have relied too much on bad advice, advertising, and hearsay, and as a result are out of funds. You will be able to rectify the situation, but let it be a warning to you to never go ahead with anything that involves money without double-checking and getting all the information first.

30-SECOND READING

Susan and her sister are arguing about a CD. Both thought it was theirs and didn't want the other to have it. The Hierophant is suggesting that Susan is too interested in material things and is forgetting the important things in life. If she would only sit down and think about it, she would see that the CD isn't nearly as important as her relationship with her sister.

6: THE LOVERS

This card celebrates love and partnership and the way both can lift you up to the heavens in terms of ecstasy and sheer joy of living. You will see the archangel Raphael on the top of this card. The archangel's hands are held out above both the man and the woman, showing that to feel whole you need to be in touch both with your doing, working (traditionally masculine) side and your sharing, caring (traditionally feminine) side. In this way the card signifies awareness of yourself as an individual, which is the first step on the road to enlightenment. The Lovers is also the card of temptation or choice—a choice between two lifestyles or two people. There could be some confusion with emotions, so look at all the pros and cons of the situation.

Questions to ask yourself if you draw The Lovers:

- Is there a new love interest in your life?
- Do you have to make a choice of some sort?
- Do you realize that until you love yourself you can't love anyone else?
- Are you coming to terms with the traditionally masculine and feminine parts of yourself?
- Is something or someone tearing you apart?
- What is making you feel good or bad about yourself?

Friends

UPSIDE: A new friend will come into your life from a different culture or religious background. Celebrate and enjoy this, as it will enrich and invigorate your life.

DOWNSIDE: You are unwilling to meet people who think differently than you do. Stop being prejudiced; you will end up leading a very limited life.

School

UPSIDE: You will find that two quite different subjects—for example music and math, or science and religion—are a lot more similar than you think. This will help you understand both better.

DOWNSIDE: If you avoid things you don't understand, you will never learn anything about anything. Have the courage to explore and make mistakes. That is the only way to learn and grow as a human being.

KEY THOUGHTS:
Put your talents to the best possible use. Until you respect and love yourself, you can't love someone else.

Dating

UPSIDE: You are very drawn to someone. Find out more about that person before you decide to take the matter further.

DOWNSIDE: Misunderstandings and jealousy threaten to break up an important relationship. An ex may reappear on the scene.

Family

UPSIDE: Adults close to you will experience a renewal of their vows of love to each other or meet a new life partner. Be happy for them.

DOWNSIDE: The arguments of adults close to you are forcing you to take sides. Try your best not to get involved, as it will only rebound on you.

Interests

UPSIDE: You are eager to experience lots of new things. It doesn't matter if you are good or bad at these things; your zest for life will be noticed and rewarded.

DOWNSIDE: You are set in your ways. This is keeping a lot of good things from coming your way.

Health/Looks

UPSIDE: You don't need any advice. You know you look good.

DOWNSIDE: Don't spend too much time obsessing about your looks. Love affairs with the mirror always end in disappointment.

Money

UPSIDE: You will find new ways to make money, and they will be thoroughly rewarding and enjoyable.

DOWNSIDE: Are you spending too much money on your friends or potential partners? You can't buy love. People have to like you not for what you can buy them, but for who you are.

30-SECOND READING

Gabriella is head over heels in love with a boy who is more interested in baseball than he is in her. She has tried everything to get his attention, but nothing seems to work. A few weeks ago she sent him a letter saying how much she liked him. Unfortunately, some of his friends read it, which was incredibly embarrassing. She can't believe he is still talking to her. The Lovers suggests that he was more flattered than embarrassed, and that if she backs off for a while he will soon be a friend, at the very least. The card also says that she needs to work on loving herself before entering into a relationship.

7: THE CHARIOT

The Chariot is the card of willpower and triumph over difficulties. You will notice that the person driving the chariot seems totally focused. He knows where he wants to go and is aiming for it with great strength and purpose. The water in the background shows that what's familiar and known to you must be left behind in order for you to grow and expand. It is time to move on. The charioteer is holding the reins of two black-and-white creatures. The black and white suggest that success and failure are two sides of the same coin, and that both are very necessary experiences in life. In fact, failure is frequently much more useful, because you can learn so much more from it than you can from success. After all, the journey of your life is to self-knowledge, and this can be found only through trial and error and the insight gained from experience.

Questions to ask yourself if you draw The Chariot:

- What are you reluctant to leave behind?
- What direction are you headed in?
- Do you feel pulled in lots of different directions?
- What are you heading toward?
- What can be learned from your mistakes?
- Are you feeling impatient?

Friends

UPSIDE: Your friends bring hope and strength to a seemingly impossible situation.

DOWNSIDE: Two friends are pulling you in two different directions. You can't be everything to everybody, so make a decision about where you stand. Peer pressure is probably an issue you need to acknowledge and deal with.

School

UPSIDE: Your focus and determination will pay off. Now is not the time to stop. Keep going and victory will be yours.

DOWNSIDE: You tend to waste time at school chatting with friends or daydreaming. Try to find out why you are doing these things. Once you find out why—perhaps you don't like pressure or are afraid that you won't do well—you can work on the real issue and concentrate on your work.

Dating

UPSIDE: No problems in this area if you just believe in yourself.
DOWNSIDE: Are you lying to yourself? Do you really want to be in a relationship right now?

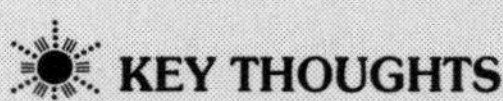
KEY THOUGHTS: You are at a turning point in your life, and nothing can ever be the same again.

Family

UPSIDE: You are a tower of strength for your family right now.
DOWNSIDE: There could be a lot of tension at home. Find out why you lose your cool. Are you just using your family to release pent-up tension? If you don't acknowledge what is upsetting you, it will never change.

Interests

UPSIDE: You are moving toward new interests that could take your life in a whole new direction. Enjoy this exciting development.
DOWNSIDE: You are reluctant to move forward with your life. Let the past go, acknowledge that life moves on, and start looking for new interests, new friendships, new passions. It is often easy to stay in a comfort zone where everything is familiar. But if you break out of that comfort zone, you will be rewarded for it.

Health/Looks

UPSIDE: Your confidence about yourself is at an all-time high. There is no one who can resist you.
DOWNSIDE: There is a difference between confidence and arrogance. Confidence is believing in yourself and respecting the needs of others. Arrogance is having a false opinion of yourself and disregarding the needs of others.

Money

UPSIDE: This card signifies wealth. You may not have it now, but one day you will, and along with it will come honor.

DOWNSIDE: Anxiety about money may keep you from enjoying it. Remember, money is nothing more than metal and paper. It is the value you give it that can create feelings of anxiety or security.

30-SECOND READING

David is eager to win a baseball match championship. The Chariot is indicating he will help his team win, provided he keeps up the level of training he is doing at the moment and works on controlling his nerves. The most important thing, win or lose, is that he does not identify himself with failure or success, but rather sees both as learning opportunities. There is no such thing as a problem-free life. Everyone, however successful, has their fair share of disappointment. The secret isn't to avoid setbacks but to learn how to manage them.

8: STRENGTH

The Lion in this card symbolizes passion, but for passion to be effective it needs to be tamed and directed. Your energy has to be transformed into strength. Sometimes it is good to follow your emotions. If you repress yourself too much this can lead to unhappiness. However, like everything in life, moderation is the key. The woman in the picture is making friends with the lion. You can only control your passions by understanding them. You will notice the figure 8 above her like a halo. This means that whatever battles you are facing in your life at the moment will pass. In years to come you may not even remember what you are worrying about now. Above all, this card signifies strength of will—doing the work that is needed to

get what you want. Don't be intimidated if something seems like an impossible challenge. It may not come easy, and there will be setbacks along the way, but keep persevering till you get what you want. Remember, you are a failure only if you don't try.

Questions to ask yourself if you draw Strength:

- What is your greatest strength? How are you directing that strength?
- Are you or is someone you know in need of tough love?
- Do you feel like you are losing, or winning?
- What would be the best way to tame a beast?
- When is your strength your weakness and your weakness your strength?
- Are you a hero or a victim?

Friends

UPSIDE: You are having a tough time with some of your friends. This is because you are maturing and moving forward with your life, and they are not. Let these friends go.

DOWNSIDE: Your wild behavior is alienating those closest to you. Take care if you want to keep your friends.

School

UPSIDE: Your hard work is paying off and producing excellent academic results. Well done! Never forget that success is 5 percent inspiration and 95 percent effort.

DOWNSIDE: Don't give up if you don't do well immediately. Eventually you will if you keep working hard.

Dating

UPSIDE: If you recently have been very hurt by someone you cared about, this card shows that your strength is returning and it won't be long before you recover fully from your disappointment.

DOWNSIDE: You may lack confidence and find it hard to meet new people. This card tells you that you will find the strength to conquer your shyness. You will be able to get out there and have some fun.

Family

UPSIDE: You are wise beyond your years and always see the best in everyone and every situation. Thanks to you, arguments in the home are kept to a minimum.

DOWNSIDE: You take delight in creating ugly scenes at home. You're not a very happy person right now. Talk to someone you trust about the way you feel.

KEY THOUGHTS:

You have the inner strength to deal with a situation well and to stand firm in the face of problems. Believe in yourself. Take action today.

Interests

UPSIDE: You are directing your energy positively in activities, like sports, that can improve both your body and mind.

DOWNSIDE: If you do nothing, you will have nothing. Looking out the window and hoping things will come your way is the language of losers. Don't be a loser. Be a winner. Get out there and find out what you are interested in.

Health/Looks

UPSIDE: Your inner strength makes you a charismatic and beautiful person.

DOWNSIDE: It might be a good idea to tone down your style. Other people may feel threatened by things like body piercing and heavy makeup. If that is your intention, be honest with yourself about why you want to look so different. It's a cliché but it is true: The only change that really matters is the change that goes on inside, not outside.

Money

UPSIDE: Money will come your way soon. Make sure you put it to good use. There may also be an offer of employment.

DOWNSIDE: You must learn to value money and use it wisely. Until you can do that you won't have much of it.

30-SECOND READING

Rona is suffering from terrible acne. For the past month or so she has stayed home most nights when her blemishes flare up because she is too embarrassed to see anyone. What can she do? Strength indicates that she has got to get over her embarrassment and live her life to the fullest again. This card offers the strength to withstand difficulties. She can do everything she can to get rid of the acne (and in time it will disappear), but she needs to know that people will react not to her blemishes but to her embarrassment about them. If she is cool about it, other people will be, too.

9: THE HERMIT

The Hermit is a symbol of wisdom in solitude, a wise teacher or inner voice that gives you good advice. The Hermit is carrying a lantern, which represents the light of knowledge lighting up the path ahead for you. The Hermit lives in solitude, and it is only by spending some time alone that you can reflect and gain wisdom, symbolized by the Hermit's staff. You may have a fear of solitude—being seen as a loner is often the biggest fear at school—but this card encourages you to follow your instinct and take the time to find out who you are. However, the reverse is also true. Sometimes people withdraw from social contact because they can't relate to those around them. Cutting yourself off in this way will only make you feel lonely and limit your potential. If you draw this card, you need to accept your individuality, not repress it. Even if you feel different from others, you still have to be yourself. Be calm, work hard, and rise above the noise and bustle around you.

Questions to ask yourself if you draw The Hermit:

- Do you spend any time alone?
- Are you withdrawing from other people too much?
- Can you be alone without feeling lonely?
- Do you sometimes feel wiser than your years?
- Is there someone who is a guiding light for you?
- Do you feel that you fit in?

Friends

UPSIDE: You are terrific. You like to do your own thing, but you also like to get involved with others. As far as friendship is concerned, you have the balance right.

DOWNSIDE: This could indicate false or shallow friendship and saying bad things about others, causing personal hurt and distress. It can also be the card of loneliness. Stop isolating yourself from others. No one is an island.

School

UPSIDE: You are wise not to write off that eccentric teacher everyone makes fun of. You can learn a lot from him or her.

DOWNSIDE: Your choices are isolating you. Lack of involvement in team activities is limiting your learning.

Dating

UPSIDE: You may find yourself attracted to someone a little older than you.

DOWNSIDE: You find it difficult to get dates. Stop trying so hard. Relax. Find things you enjoy and sooner or later you will find someone attracted to you not because you are seeking a partner but because you are enjoying your life.

KEY THOUGHTS:

Have the courage to be yourself and go it alone if you have to.

Family

UPSIDE: Your family respects you and admires your individuality.

DOWNSIDE: Part of you may be refusing to grow up and see your family and the world as they really are. Your parents aren't perfect; they are human just like everybody else.

Interests

UPSIDE: Solitary pursuits, like chess or computers, appeal to you. In moderation they will give you a lot.

DOWNSIDE: Don't spend all your free time alone. Other people would love to get to know you and share some of your interests.

Health/Looks

UPSIDE: You are one of those people who look younger than your years. You may not like it now, but in years to come your youthful looks will be the envy of your peer group.

DOWNSIDE: You are stuck in a style rut and fearful of innovation and change. Try experimenting a bit with your personal style. Try a new hairstyle or a new look.

Money

UPSIDE: You are very careful with money and will never spend more than you earn.

DOWNSIDE: Excessive caution with money can keep you from having fun. Try to get the balance.

30-SECOND READING

Susie is bulimic. She does everything she can to avoid mealtimes and forces herself to vomit regularly. It all started when a friend told her she was fat. What can she do? The Hermit, the card for eating disorders, is telling her that if she carries on in her present path, there will be nothing but unhappiness. It is crucial for her to seek help from her doctor. Eating disorders are an illness and require medical help.

10: THE WHEEL OF FORTUNE

The Wheel of Fortune is the card of change. It suggests the beginning of a new cycle. You are not the same you as the you that started middle school a few years back, or even the same you that got up this morning. As life constantly changes, it is important not to get too wrapped up in your current problems. They will pass and be replaced by other challenges. Nothing stays the same, and it is often the case that things that appear bad now may actually be seen as good when you look back in a few years' time. The circle in the center of the card shows that all life is a circle and in some sense constantly repeats itself. Think of the seasons of nature, and of youth giving way to old age and then the next generation. The passing of the old is necessary to bring in the new. Some people see this card as being about karma—you reap what you sow. Others see it as accepting that life is about constant change. There is nothing we can do about change, so we may as well adapt to it and enjoy it.

Questions to ask yourself if you draw the Wheel of Fortune:

- What cycle are you completing or ending—a school year, another birthday coming up, and so on?
- How well do you cope with change?
- Do you have lots of emotional ups and downs?
- What is turning your life around?
- Are you experiencing the fallout or the rewards from some past action?
- How could you become more aligned to changes?

Friends

UPSIDE: New friends are coming into your life. Their energy will lift and energize you.

DOWNSIDE: Stop holding on to past friendships. Let them go. You have outgrown them.

School

UPSIDE: Everything is falling into place. Subjects you found difficult you are now starting to enjoy.

DOWNSIDE: You are starting to fail in subjects you once did well in. Think about what you can do to reverse that trend.

Dating

UPSIDE: A stimulating new love interest is on the horizon.

DOWNSIDE: You are having a run of bad luck in your relationships. Think about how you may be contributing to the situation. Perhaps there is something else, school or family or friends, that you should be concentrating on right now.

Family

UPSIDE: Family income and circumstances change for the better. You could be moving to a different house. Enjoy the new lifestyle.

DOWNSIDE: Your family has far less money to spend than in the past. Do your part to cut back.

Interests

UPSIDE: New interests come your way, and they will help you with your future career.

DOWNSIDE: Have you outgrown some of your hobbies or interests? Is it time to strike out in new areas?

Health/Looks

UPSIDE: You always keep up with current fashions and trends. You are one cool-looking kid.

DOWNSIDE: There is a difference between being fashionable and becoming a slave to fashion. The former is about dressing to express who you are; the latter is about dressing to impress other people. Don't be a follower. Be a leader.

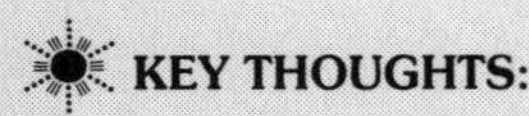

KEY THOUGHTS:

You have an opportunity now to begin again and make a fresh start. Stop making excuses, and start winning.

Money

UPSIDE: You may have to work hard for your extra cash, but this helps you appreciate it more and gives you a sense of independence.

DOWNSIDE: It might be wise for you to avoid any kind of gambling for the time being. Instead of waiting for money to come to you the easy way, find ways you can earn it.

30-SECOND READING

Alan is trying to get a part-time job but has had no luck yet. The Wheel of Fortune indicates that his present poverty will not last long. At the moment he has no money and so is at the bottom of the cycle, but things are bound to change as the wheel moves upward. His determination and willingness to work for what he wants will pay off soon, and his finances will improve.

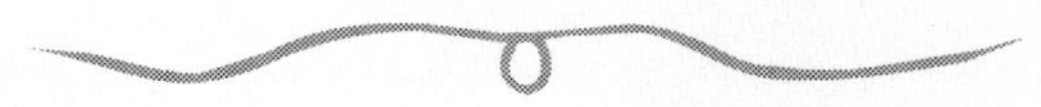

11: JUSTICE

In this picture we see Justice holding her scales. This indicates how important it is to carefully weigh the consequences of your decisions. Justice also carries a sword of discernment. After deciding that you are willing to take responsibility for your actions, all you can do is act in good faith. Sometimes it may be possible to rebalance a difficult situation, but other times it may not. This is the card of personal decisions. We are held accountable for our own actions, and the truth will be revealed. Do what is right for you, not what others want you to do. Central to this card is the idea of taking responsibility for things within your control (schoolwork, for example) and not blaming yourself for what is out of your control (your parents' divorce, for example), and having the wisdom to know the difference.

Questions to ask yourself if you draw Justice:

- Are you taking responsibility for your actions?
- Is something throwing you off balance?
- Are you trying to change things that are out of your control?
- Do you need to weigh the pros and cons of a situation?
- Is something unjust upsetting you?
- Are you in a period of readjustment?

Friends

UPSIDE: You are the kind of person who stands up for the underdog. Even though your friends may tease you about this, secretly they will admire and respect you.

DOWNSIDE: All that gossiping about others is starting to rebound. People don't trust you anymore, and you need to make a real effort to regain that trust.

KEY THOUGHTS:

Don't take anything at face value. Search deep within yourself to discover the truth. Be decisive and fight for what you believe in.

School

UPSIDE: Progress in academic work is like building a house. It is constructed brick by brick. You have built secure foundations, and are now reaping the benefits.

DOWNSIDE: If you don't put in the effort, don't be surprised if you see poor results. Your teachers are not to blame. You are.

Dating

UPSIDE: Whatever you have, it's a shame they can't bottle and sell it. You are a people magnet.

DOWNSIDE: Someone you are close to will enjoy a string of successes. Stop feeling insecure and jealous, and find your own success.

Family

UPSIDE: Your family may be facing a court case or something of a legal nature. There will be a good outcome.

DOWNSIDE: There may be disappointment in legal or financial matters.

Interests

UPSIDE: You are showing an interest in the law and debating. Keep it up. This could be the career of your choice one day.

DOWNSIDE: Getting involved in illegal interests will put you on the wrong side of the law.

Health/Looks

UPSIDE: If you want to look good, it's up to you. Put in the time and make the effort. It will pay off.

DOWNSIDE: All those late nights, fast food, and fast living are starting to catch up with you. Start thinking about making healthy changes in your lifestyle.

Money

UPSIDE: The job or career you are thinking about will bring financial reward in time.

DOWNSIDE: You are now or will soon be in debt if you don't start to think before you spend.

30-SECOND READING

Simon is being bullied. His classmates have all grown taller than he is, and he's now the smallest boy in the class. He is fed up with being called "Shorty" and can't defend himself against the bigger boys. The Justice card means that he should not hesitate to tell his teachers about the situation to ensure that justice is done so he'll feel safe at school. The bullies will be warned to leave him alone, and he will be able to enjoy life again.

12: THE HANGED MAN

The Hanged Man card advises rest and reflection. You will notice the hanged man has a halo and white hair, both of which symbolize wisdom. He doesn't look as if he is uncomfortable and seems to be enjoying his rest. Despite being tied, his legs hang freely, suggesting that his attitude toward life is free and he can, if he wants to, walk away. He looks comfortable and is biding his time, waiting for the right moment. The Hanged Man is also upside down, which suggests that sometimes we need to look at things from a different perspective in order to learn lessons. His legs point to heaven, signifying the purity of his intentions (this is also the card of self-sacrifice for the good of others) and the wonderful things that lie in store for him when he returns to action.

Questions to ask yourself if you draw The Hanged Man:

- Do you need to take some time to think about things?
- Are you putting your plans on hold?
- Why are you hung up?
- Are you looking at things in a totally different way?
- Are you surrendering yourself to a higher cause, like politics or medicine?
- Is something restricting you?

Friends

UPSIDE: People love to be around you because you are laid-back and willing to put your needs aside for the good of everyone else.

DOWNSIDE: You are drifting a little and not setting boundaries in your relationships. This will eventually lead to resentment on both sides.

School

UPSIDE: You are thinking about what different subjects can teach you, not just in terms of exam grades but also in how they will help you make your contribution to the world.

DOWNSIDE: You need to concentrate right now. You are being given valuable information that you won't have time to work through again.

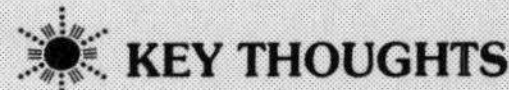

KEY THOUGHTS:

A turning point has been reached. Something may be lost, but something will also be gained. Remember, when one door closes another always opens.

Dating

UPSIDE: You don't have to do much; love comes knocking at your door. It must be because you are so relaxed about life and easy to approach.

DOWNSIDE: If you don't make an effort with your relationship, it will fall apart. If someone is special to you, don't let selfishness destroy what you have together.

Family

UPSIDE: You are getting a lot of help and support from your family.

DOWNSIDE: Don't sacrifice yourself for the sake of someone else in your family. Do offer to help, of course, but not at your own expense.

Interests

UPSIDE: You are getting a reputation as quite a philosopher. People love to hear what you have to say about life, the universe, and everything else.

DOWNSIDE: Stop saying you are bored all the time. Everything is interesting if you make an effort. If you are bored, it could be because you are becoming boring yourself.

Health/Looks

UPSIDE: You are comfortable with the way you look, and this makes you attractive to others.

DOWNSIDE: You are longing to look more grown-up. Take it slow. Before you know it, you'll be grown-up and longing to look young again!

Money

UPSIDE: You are good at saving money, and this quality can give you stability in the midst of instability.

DOWNSIDE: You have a generous nature but must make sure you don't become a martyr and give away too much to other people.

30-SECOND READING

Hassan's friend Joe is taking drugs. Joe is falling behind at school and is now pressuring Hassan to take drugs, too. Hassan is worried that if he refuses to take them he will lose a friend. The Hanged Man shows how drugs can make you lazy and uninvolved in what is going on around you. The card is saying that very soon Hassan could be like this, too, unless he takes positive action. He should not take the drugs and also should not ignore what he is seeing. He should talk to an adult he trusts to see what can be done to help Joe.

13: DEATH

The Death card is the one that sends shivers down your spine, but it really isn't as scary as it looks. The Death card actually represents change, and change can be a liberating experience. This card is telling you to ditch old ways of doing things or old thought patterns that are holding you back and keeping you from getting new opportunities. The sun rises in the east, showing that death is as much a part of life as the sun setting and rising every day. The skeletal figure sits upon a horse. The horse is white to show that death or change should not be feared. We see the horse trampling all before it—kings, priests, children, and maidens—suggesting that change affects everybody, whether rich or poor. This card doesn't usually mean an actual death, but the death of an old self or way of doing things. It is the card of transformation and change.

Questions to ask yourself if you draw the Death card:

- What don't you want to let go of?
- Are you looking forward to becoming an adult?
- What or who are you missing?
- What worn-out ways of thinking and living are you being forced to drop?
- Is it time to forget the old and begin the new?
- Is there someone or something you need to say goodbye to?

Friends

UPSIDE: You are full of new ideas, and your friends can only benefit from your enthusiasm and energy.

DOWNSIDE: You are holding on to old friendships that worked several years ago but don't work now. It is time to meet new people and move on.

School

UPSIDE: You are taking responsibility for your learning rather than waiting for the teacher to spoon-feed you. Well done.

DOWNSIDE: You are avoiding subjects that will challenge you and introduce you to new ideas. Taking the easy way is never the best policy. You will regret it.

Dating

UPSIDE: You are growing up fast and need to find a partner who is as mature as you are and is on your wavelength.

DOWNSIDE: A relationship is breaking up, or you are losing interest in someone you thought you liked. This will be a good thing in the long run.

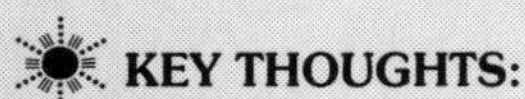

KEY THOUGHTS:

Sometimes unwelcome change can be a blessing in disguise, because it clears the way for something better. This is a time for new beginnings or a fresh start.

Family

UPSIDE: You are being given added responsibility in your family. This is because you have demonstrated to them how mature and responsible you can be.

DOWNSIDE: A recent loss, disappointment, or bereavement has upset everybody. Be kind to yourself and others at this trying time.

Interests

UPSIDE: You will find detective and murder mystery books and programs interesting. Studying human behavior can help you understand yourself better.

DOWNSIDE: Your old interests aren't inspiring you anymore. Leave them behind, and find new ways to fill your spare time.

Health/Looks

UPSIDE: You look in the mirror and you don't see a boy or a girl anymore—you see a man or a woman. You like what you see.

DOWNSIDE: You look in the mirror and see someone you don't recognize. You need to find ways to build your self-confidence.

Money

UPSIDE: You accept that it will be a while before you can earn the kind of money you would like, and you make the best of your situation.

DOWNSIDE: You have unrealistic expectations about your earning potential.

30-SECOND READING

Tim is worrying everybody. Recently he was taken into custody and released without charge on suspicion of breaking a shop window. The Death card for Tim does not indicate actual death; what it says is that Tim is currently in a negative situation, which will continue to spiral downward until he can change his attitude. If he resists change now, life will get harder and harder for him. His current mindset must change, must die away, if he is to move forward with his life.

14: TEMPERANCE

Temperance generally indicates good fortune when it appears in a spread. The angel represents moderation and an avoidance of extremes in anything. This is the card of calm, compromise, moderation, and choosing the middle path—the ability to adapt and be patient if need be. We see the angel pouring water from one cup to another, showing how quickly one experience gives way to another. The cups mix the seemingly contradictory elements of the spirit world and the real world, but we can see in the picture that they are one and the same. This halfway house between two things can also be seen by the way the angel is standing. One foot is on land and one is on water; land represents the solid and practical, water the intuitive and spiritual. The card suggests that happiness can be found when we get the balance in our lives right.

Questions to ask yourself if you draw Temperance:

- Have you been under stress lately?
- Are there conflicting interests in your life?
- Are you in need of guidance?
- Are you a person of extremes, or do you keep your feet firmly on the ground?
- What is working in your life? What isn't working?
- Do you have a good balance between work, rest, and play?

Friends

UPSIDE: Your common sense is keeping some of your friends from getting themselves into trouble. They might not thank you now, but they will thank you in the long run.
DOWNSIDE: Stop sitting on the fence all the time. If you never have an opinion, people may start to ignore you.

School

UPSIDE: You are pacing yourself well in your studies. You are not getting stressed by them, but neither are you being lazy. Give yourself a pat on the back.
DOWNSIDE: Are you concentrating too much on one subject or activity at school at the expense of all the others?

Dating

UPSIDE: You are in a good relationship, but don't forget that there are other things in your life besides romance.
DOWNSIDE: You are way overinvolved with your partner or obsessing about a potential partner. Get some balance back in your life.

Family

UPSIDE: Your sound and wise advice has calmed what could have been an explosive and dangerous situation. Well done!

DOWNSIDE: Don't lose all sense of yourself in difficult family dynamics.

Interests

UPSIDE: You enjoy reading, and this will stand you in good stead later in life.

DOWNSIDE: Have you been struggling with any drug, alcohol, or food addictions? Stop doing things that harm you, and get advice and help from someone you trust.

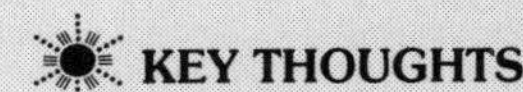

Experience life in a calm frame of mind. Take control of yourself, and learn to compromise and cooperate.

Health/Looks

UPSIDE: You always look relaxed, happy, and fulfilled. Other people may try to copy your personal style.

DOWNSIDE: You could have an unhealthy attitude toward food or be doing something that isn't going to benefit your looks in the long term—for example, smoking. If you want to look good you have to start making healthy changes in your lifestyle right now.

Money

UPSIDE: Money is important to you, but so are the people and things you love. You have the right attitude about money. You value it, but you don't crave it.

DOWNSIDE: Don't let your need for money lead you down a dangerous path. Remember, every action has a consequence.

30-SECOND READING

Monesha loves ice-skating. She has been accepted for a class that could give her the training she needs to skate professionally. The class starts next year, which seems a very long time to

(continued)

Monesha. She would like to quit school and start right now. Temperance is saying that she needs to be patient. Everything will happen in the fullness of time.

15: THE DEVIL

The Devil suggests disappointment, limited opportunities, and inner fears we do not acknowledge. It can also mean an unhealthy fixation on either sex or money. The Devil sits on a tiny cube that is clearly too small for him, symbolizing the discomfort he feels with his limited vision of life. The humans on the card, however, look quite content. Sometimes when you are in a bad situation it's easy to make yourself believe that it is acceptable. It's only when you realize that things aren't working that the discomfort shows. The chains are quite loose, showing that situations can be changed and are not the burdens you think they are. For example, if you have a drinking problem, you can do something about it. But you can only change a negative situation if you have the determination and maturity to do so. When The Devil appears in a spread it often indicates that the kind of maturity needed to rise above conflict has yet to come. On the other hand, it can also suggest a need to come to terms with your immaturity or to follow your instincts. Accepting your humanity—with its limitations—can free you from the bondage of self-hatred.

Questions to ask yourself if you draw The Devil:

- Are you too concerned about material things?
- Do you feel powerless over sexual urges or addictive behavior?
- Are you intentionally upsetting or harming someone else?
- What are your instincts telling you to do? Should you follow them?
- Are you trying too hard to be perfect?
- Do you sometimes feel guilty and ashamed of yourself?

Friends

UPSIDE: Some of your friends are getting involved in potentially dangerous situations, for example where drink or drugs are involved. Your help and guidance at this point could prove crucial.

DOWNSIDE: You and your friends are behaving in an immature way. Now is a good time to think about constructive and positive ways to use your time.

School

UPSIDE: You may be involved in or be witnessing bullying and taunting at your school. It is important that you talk to teachers in confidence about it.

DOWNSIDE: Making people laugh now and again is cool, but joking around all the time isn't. Stop trying so hard to please other people.

Dating

UPSIDE: If you don't feel ready for sex but your boyfriend or girlfriend is demanding it, stand your ground. Don't on any account be pressured into doing something you don't want to do. You will regret it.

DOWNSIDE: Are you thinking about sex all the time? Are you sleeping around? If you are, look again at the devil on the card. Too much of one thing isn't good for you.

Family

UPSIDE: It's possible that someone in your household has a secret or is feeling depressed. They should seek professional help.

DOWNSIDE: If anyone close to you is encouraging you to do things you don't want to do or is treating you in a way that demeans you, make sure you talk to and seek advice from an adult you trust.

KEY THOUGHTS:

You may feel you are stuck in a negative situation, but there is a solution to the problem that you have not yet seen. Your challenge is to take responsibility for your problems, stop blaming other people or things, and have the courage to break free.

Interests

UPSIDE: You have a clear idea about what interests you and what does not. You have the maturity to stay away from activities that you know are harmful or dangerous.

DOWNSIDE: You could be wasting your time with leisure pursuits that cost a lot of money but don't do you any good—drugs or pornography, for example. Stop using them as a substitute for having a life.

Health/Looks

UPSIDE: You have the kind of looks that appeal to everyone. You ooze sex appeal.

DOWNSIDE: Are you treating your body with respect? Body piercing and tattoos in moderation are okay, but in excess they can be a form of self-harm.

Money

UPSIDE: You enjoy spending money and love the good things in life. Nothing gives you more pleasure than an afternoon spent shopping or buying presents for the people you love.

DOWNSIDE: Don't fall too deeply in love with money. It is easy to feel imprisoned by the material world.

30-SECOND READING

Thomas is feeling down. He is overweight and doesn't feel he has much to offer any of the people in his class. During breaks in his schedule, he avoids everyone and sits in the library. The Devil is the card of negativity. Thomas is caught in a negative way of thinking. He is putting himself in his own prison. Drawing this card suggests that he needs to change his attitude and seek support from his parents/guardians or from his doctor.

16: THE TOWER

This card depicts the Tower of Babel. According to the Bible, the people of the world decided to work together to build a tower that would reach the sky and be more magnificent than God. At that time all the people of the world spoke one language. When God found out about the tower, he got angry and punished the people by scattering them to different places, and forcing them to speak different languages so that nobody could understand what anyone else was saying. Then God destroyed the tower. This story explains the origin of the thousands of languages the world speaks today. This card shows how concentrating too much on money or worldly success or your ego will always prove to be hollow, and then everything will come crashing down around you. It is a card of destructiveness and sudden, violent change. This doesn't have to be a change in outward circumstances; it can also be an inner change—a sudden realization or awareness that shatters your long-held beliefs. At the time it is painful, but in the long run it will lead to greater understanding and wisdom. This card is saying, "Don't be afraid of a dramatic change you can't avoid. There will be a positive reason for it that you understand later."

Questions to ask yourself if you draw The Tower:

- Do you feel as if your life is falling apart?
- Are you overstepping your boundaries?
- Has some natural disaster or accident affected you deeply?
- What must fall down in order for something better to replace it?
- What needs restructuring?
- Do you feel as if you are about to explode?

Friends

UPSIDE: Your circle of friends is about to change. You will suddenly realize who your real friends are.

DOWNSIDE: Your friends are turning their backs on you. Stop worrying about it, and find new friends.

KEY THOUGHTS:

Break out of your shell. Make necessary changes. The stage is set for a change for the better.

School

UPSIDE: Your studies are about to take you into a completely new direction. There will be a noticeable improvement in your results.

DOWNSIDE: Poor results at school are damaging your self-confidence. You aren't sure what you are doing wrong, and you need to seek advice from your teacher.

Dating

UPSIDE: You will learn something about someone you like that will completely change your perception of them.

DOWNSIDE: A relationship could end suddenly and cause you a great deal of pain and upset.

Family

UPSIDE: There is likely to be a great deal of change on the home front. You may be moving to a new house, a new state, or even to a new country. Although you feel unsettled at the moment, in the long run these changes will be for the best.

DOWNSIDE: The same tensions and stresses keep repeating over and over again at home. A new approach is needed if the situation is to change for the better.

Interests

UPSIDE: You are getting bored with your activities outside school and home. It is time to find new interests and meet new people.

DOWNSIDE: You are hanging on to someone or something in your life that isn't doing you any good. Don't let this drag you down any more.

Health/Looks

UPSIDE: You are about to drastically change your appearance. Your new look will give you renewed confidence in yourself.

DOWNSIDE: If you think you are unattractive you will never be attractive. Stop criticizing your appearance, and start looking for the positive. The secret to being beautiful is not the way you look, but the way you feel about yourself.

Money

UPSIDE: You will avoid getting into debt by handling a potentially difficult situation well.

DOWNSIDE: If you need financial help, you have to ask for it or, better still, find ways to earn it. Don't let your pride get you into debt.

30-SECOND READING

Tina is upset because her boyfriend has been sleeping with her best friend. She feels betrayed. Everything she holds dear has come crashing around her. The Tower acknowledges the pain Tina feels, but it also shows that although one chapter in her life has ended, another has opened up. This new chapter will bring many wonderful and happy surprises.

17: THE STAR

In The Star card a woman pours water freely. This symbolizes creativity, for true creativity never runs dry. Think about the times you suddenly got an idea for a picture, song, or story. You could have gone on for hours and were full of energy. The colors in the card are bright, suggesting the sparkle and joy of new pursuits. The woman is naked and completely unconscious of her nakedness, which shows her joy in living. She has one foot in the water and one foot on the land to indicate that she is both practical (earth) and spiritual (water). She sees the beauty and wonder of the universe all around her and lives in a world of hope and peace. This card is the card of hope, inspiration, and optimism.

Questions to ask yourself if you draw The Star:

- Are you the star of your own life?
- What are you hoping for?
- What are you asking for?
- Are you being honest about what you need and who you are?
- What hope can you see in a difficult situation?
- Are you afraid of the future?

Friends

UPSIDE: You bring hope and inspiration to your friendships. Your positive attitude and love of life encourages your friends to see the good in themselves.

DOWNSIDE: You are not being honest with your friends. Take a moment to reflect. Don't you want your friends to like you for who you are?

KEY THOUGHTS:
Seize the moment and enjoy yourself. You will be guided to the next stage in your life.

School

UPSIDE: You are drawn toward religious and ethical studies. Now is the time to start incorporating some of the insights that you are gaining into your life.

DOWNSIDE: You are having problems with creativity. Find ways to stimulate your imagination. Read more, listen to others, experience new things.

Dating

UPSIDE: You and your partner have something quite magical together. Enjoy this very special time. If you don't have a partner and have set your sights on someone you think is unattainable, reach for the impossible dream and ask this person out.

DOWNSIDE: There is a lot of confusion in your mind about what you do and do not want in a relationship. You may need some time alone to sort things out in your mind.

Family

UPSIDE: A much-needed period of peace and calm lies ahead for all your family.
DOWNSIDE: Stress levels are high with your family. You would all benefit from a vacation or some quiet time together.

Interests

UPSIDE: You have started to get interested in a whole range of religions, both mainstream and alternative. This is just the start of your journey toward self-knowledge and fulfillment.
DOWNSIDE: You are too influenced by celebrities. Remember, these people aren't real. They are always projecting a certain image, and what you see is not who they are.

Health/Looks

UPSIDE: You don't tend to worry much about the way you look and have an effortless natural charm about you. Wherever you go, you shine like a star.
DOWNSIDE: You like to camouflage yourself whenever you are with other people. Stop trying to hide, and let the world see how beautiful you are.

Money

UPSIDE: Financial success is not your main aim in life. You are far more concerned with spiritual and emotional fulfillment.
DOWNSIDE: You cannot live on love alone. We all need to eat and pay our way. Make sure you pay attention to your physical needs as well as your emotional and spiritual ones.

30-SECOND READING

Sonia wants to be a lawyer. She is wondering if she has what it takes to be a lawyer or if she should settle for something less ambitious. The Star is telling her to go after her dream. The prospects for success are very bright. She will have to work hard, but it will pay off in the end.

18: THE MOON

The Moon is the card of imagination and dreams, the twilight time between sleep and waking. Imagination is a wonderful thing, but it needs to be disciplined so that it doesn't run wild. The Latin for moon is *luna,* and the connection with the word *lunatic* is obvious. In the card we see a crayfish coming out of the ocean, where all life is thought to have begun. A wolf and a dog bay at the moon, reminding us of the wild, uncivilized part of our nature. A gateway is in the distance. Gateways are symbols of entering another world, in this case the world of higher consciousness or spirit. The Moon is full of ambiguity. Everything is in half-light. You can't really see what is going on. The way you see the world is based on the pictures you create, or the lenses through which you see things. Remember, you can change your lenses or the way you look at things.

Questions to ask yourself if you draw The Moon:

- Have you been deceiving yourself?
- Do you feel confused?
- Do you feel like you are heading into the unknown?
- Have you gotten carried away with something or someone?
- Is it time to forgive yourself or someone else?
- Is everything what it seems?

Friends

UPSIDE: You are a perceptive and sensitive friend whom others feel they can trust and rely on.

DOWNSIDE: You are getting carried away with your interest in the spiritual. Remember the universal law: everything in moderation.

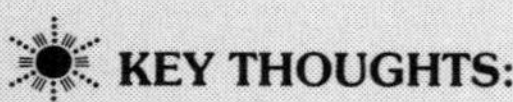

You are the only person who can change the way you see yourself and your life. Replace any confusion and uncertainty with focus and direction.

School

UPSIDE: Your school friends are very important to you at the moment. They have a positive influence on you and motivate you to do your very best.

DOWNSIDE: Too many late nights are affecting your work at school. Get your priorities sorted out. Without a decent education you won't have the fulfilling life you deserve to have.

Dating

UPSIDE: You are heading into unknown territory at the moment and thinking of going out with someone who isn't usually your type. Enjoy the experience. It will prove to be quite exciting.

DOWNSIDE: You are deceiving yourself about what is really going on in your relationship.

Family

UPSIDE: Your family is working together to create a happy, loving environment at home. Your contribution is a vital ingredient.

DOWNSIDE: A past hurt is still festering within your family. It is time to move forward, not constantly look back.

Interests

UPSIDE: Something is confusing you. Before you make any decisions, get advice, seek out information and weigh the pros and cons.

DOWNSIDE: Stay away from drugs and alcohol. They will mess with your head, heart, and soul.

Health/Looks

UPSIDE: You are very imaginative in your personal style, and people often copy the trends you set.

DOWNSIDE: It might be time to reconsider some of the more bizarre and outlandish outfits you have. Stay away from crazy diets. This is not the way to get slim or look fit. Eat more healthful food, not less, and get more exercise instead of dieting.

Money

UPSIDE: Finances look a little uncertain at the moment, but if you keep a clear head you will be able to rectify the situation.

DOWNSIDE: Avoid any kind of moneymaking scheme that sounds too good to be true. It is.

30-SECOND READING

Jonathan tends to drink late at night with his friends in the mall and has been noticed by local policemen. The Moon suggests that Jonathan is confused and in need of guidance. If he carries on drinking, his distorted sense of reality could lead to severe problems in the future.

19: THE SUN

The Sun is a happy, optimistic card that symbolizes the joy and magic in everyday life. You will notice that the child is riding bareback on a horse, which shows he is in control of his animal instincts. If you look closely you will see that the child has the body of an adult, so what we have here is the joy and simplicity of a young child combined with the mind of the adult. There is a wall in the background, which signifies obstacles that have been overcome. Flowers and abundance are everywhere, reinforcing the happy nature of the card. Energy and enthusiasm are written all over this card. The clouds disappear from life, and there is joy as the sun comes out and warms our lives.

Questions to ask yourself if you draw The Sun:

- What fills you with joy?
- Are your energy and enthusiasm helping others?
- Are you starting to like yourself?
- What success are you enjoying?
- Do you see beauty in the world around you?

Friends

UPSIDE: Your energy and enthusiasm inspire those around you.
DOWNSIDE: You are confused about some of your friendships and not sure who is trustworthy.

School

UPSIDE: You are doing particularly well in sports and/or practical subjects.
DOWNSIDE: Take care that your high energy levels don't lead to burnout.

Dating

UPSIDE: You are irresistible at the moment. The whole world loves you.

DOWNSIDE: You are being too intense at the moment. Lighten up a little bit.

Family

UPSIDE: Life is good. You will probably look back someday and think of this as one of the happiest times in your life.

DOWNSIDE: There seem to be some difficult issues with fathers or authority issues to work through.

Interests

UPSIDE: Sports interest you considerably. With the mood you're in at the moment, you could run the one-minute mile in record time.

DOWNSIDE: You have a lot of energy, but it isn't being directed well. Focus on one thing at a time.

Health/Looks

UPSIDE: You feel great about yourself. For the first time you can remember, you look in the mirror and like what you see.

DOWNSIDE: Stop being so critical of your looks. Try concentrating on what you like about yourself, not on what you don't like. If you can't find anything that you like, talk to your parents/ guardians, friends, or teachers about your feelings of self-hatred.

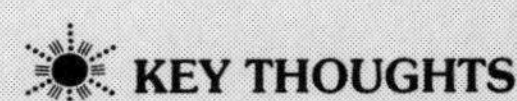

Be alert to opportunities, and trust that for you the sun will always shine.

Money

UPSIDE: You have finally learned to appreciate money, and with that appreciation money seems to come to you.

DOWNSIDE: Don't become too mean about money. A little generosity toward yourself and others now and again is a good thing.

30-SECOND READING

Alana loves to sing and dance. Her school is putting on a production of *The Wizard of Oz*, and even though she appears confident about the auditions, she wonders if she is good enough. The Sun is telling her to go for it. She will love every minute of it. Who knows? With such a positive card as The Sun, she might even end up playing Dorothy.

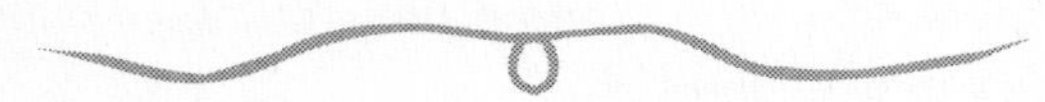

20: JUDGEMENT

The Judgment card always indicates change. This can mean looking at what you are already doing in a new way, or it could mean a complete change, like moving to another school. The angel Gabriel is blowing a trumpet and calling out to all those who hear it. The mountains in the background suggest eternal truth, and the coffins the people step out of represent their past. The people at the front of the picture are not facing us, suggesting that their knowledge so far is incomplete and there is much more for them to learn and experience. The moment has come for them to leave the past behind and create their future by either changing their perspective or changing their lives in some way. This card suggests a new lease on life, a return to health, new trends, opportunities, and challenges. When this card appears in a reading it says that regardless of the nature of the problem facing you, you can cope if you are willing to work at it. Successful people aren't successful because they don't have problems.

They are successful because they acknowledge their problems and know how to deal with them.

Questions to ask yourself if you draw Judgement:

- Are you experiencing a lot of change at present?
- What do you want to change about yourself?
- What do you want to change about your life?
- Is somebody judging you?
- Who are you passing judgment upon?
- Do you enjoy change, or does it unsettle you?

Friends

UPSIDE: You are helping those around you look at their problems in a different way. This can only be for the good.
DOWNSIDE: Stop passing judgment on those around you. Who gave you the right to be judge and jury? Forgiveness is a choice you can make. Holding on to previous hurts poisons relationships.

School

UPSIDE: Now is the time when you are rewarded for all the hard work you have put into your studies.
DOWNSIDE: Listen to your teachers; they are trying to help you.

Dating

UPSIDE: You are thinking about dating in a whole new way. It isn't something to be anxious about but something magical and liberating. It's fun.
DOWNSIDE: You are holding yourself back with self-limiting beliefs. Change the way you think about yourself, and you can change your life.

Family

UPSIDE: There are some very wise people in your family. You are learning a great deal from them.

DOWNSIDE: Stop holding on to grudges and past hurts. It isn't doing you any good. Forgiveness is a choice you can make.

Interests

UPSIDE: You are or will soon be getting involved in a worthy group effort to bring about environmental, social, and political change.

DOWNSIDE: You are getting a little too self-absorbed. There is a big wide world out there. Go exploring.

KEY THOUGHTS:

You reap what you sow. Look forward to being rewarded for past efforts. If you feel you are being dragged down by hatred and bitterness, take your power back to where it belongs—with you. Life moves on. Move with it.

Health/Looks

UPSIDE: You are finally beginning to understand that good health and good looks start from the inside.

DOWNSIDE: Obsessive dieting or exercising won't improve your looks; they will damage them.

Money

UPSIDE: You have finally repaid, or soon will repay, your debts. The relief you feel is enormous.

DOWNSIDE: Don't let other people encourage you to spend more than you earn.

30-SECOND READING

Trisha felt that her English teacher was picking on her. Yesterday Trisha swore and ran out of the classroom. She knows that when she goes into school tomorrow there are going to be problems. Judgement is saying that she didn't behave in the best possible way and will have to accept the consequences. As long as she feels that she is being treated differently from everyone else, the situation will keep on repeating itself. It is important that she talk to her English teacher about these feelings.

21: THE WORLD

The World is the card of fulfillment, but this fulfillment has to be earned. It shows a culmination of hard work and obstacles overcome. The dancer in the card dances with the universe. She goes with the flow and doesn't fight it. She is content and understands what is going on around her. There are four figureheads on the card, and these represent the various elements and responsibilities of the world. The dancer is serving all of these, which shows that by honoring your responsibilities you master worldly life and gain spiritual freedom, shown by the victory wreath. This is in many ways the most mysterious of all the cards. It suggests spiritual awakening and total fulfillment as a human being.

Questions to ask yourself if you draw The World:

- Do you feel like dancing?
- Are you celebrating something?
- Are you accepting your day-to-day responsibilities?
- Do you feel free?
- Are you disciplined enough?
- Are you enjoying your life?

Friends

UPSIDE: You accept and value your friends and don't feel the need to try to change them. Your go-with-the-flow attitude brings you many friends.

DOWNSIDE: You are reluctant to make new friends, but these new friends could have a positive influence on you.

School

UPSIDE: Your hard work is paying off. Are you or could you be near the top of the class?

DOWNSIDE: You are feeling very tied down by your workload. Try to think about it in a different way. The knowledge you are gaining now will eventually give you the freedom to lead the kind of life you want.

KEY THOUGHTS:

An inner awareness comes suddenly, bringing with it a sense of joy and fulfillment. Treat yourself well so others will be motivated to do the same. Be true to yourself, and your true needs and desires will become clear to you. Winners in life know what they want. Do you? You can be a winner. It's up to you.

Dating

UPSIDE: You will be celebrating many anniversaries with your boyfriend or girlfriend. If you don't have a partner, you will be enjoying your freedom and sense of independence.

DOWNSIDE: You can be really petty with those close to you at times. Stop sweating the small stuff. It really isn't worth it.

Family

UPSIDE: You have been making a superhuman effort to help your family recently. You will soon see that your efforts will pay off.

DOWNSIDE: Your parents are not perfect, and neither are you. Stop criticizing all the time, and look for the good rather than the bad in the people you love.

Interests

UPSIDE: Opportunities spring up all over the place, especially those involving sports or dance. How you love to move!

DOWNSIDE: Stop sitting still all the time. It isn't doing you any good. Move around more.

Health/Looks

UPSIDE: After years of hating the way you look, you are finally feeling good about yourself.

DOWNSIDE: If you don't feel good about your body, get an action plan in place to exercise more and eat more healthful food. It won't be long before you see positive results.

Money

UPSIDE: Your hard work has paid off, and you will soon have more money than you are used to.

DOWNSIDE: Stop complaining about having no money. Find ways to earn it.

30-SECOND READING

Boma has recently lost her mother to cancer. Earlier this year her dad lost his job. Boma has been through a lot—much more than many people older than she. The World tells her that bad things often happen to good people, and that the world isn't always a fair place. It also tells her that she is handling the situation well and showing a wisdom beyond her years. Her inner strength will not go unnoticed, and in time she will find the happiness she deserves.

9
Your Soul, Personality, Year, and Day Cards

Before we launch into the remaining fifty-six Tarot cards, let's have some fun with the Major Arcana and find the card that represents your soul and your personality. Once you've found out what these cards are, you might want to take some time to study them in more detail and reflect on what they may be trying to tell you about yourself. We'll also show you how you can work out what your card for this year, month, week, or day is. If you like, you can also find cards for other people: your friends, family, the guy or girl you like—even Britney Spears or Brad Pitt.

You don't need to know how to interpret the Tarot cards at this point. You just need to be good at adding up a few simple sums.

Finding Your Soul Card

Your soul card represents who you really are, not who your parents, friends, and teachers think you are.

To find your soul card, add the month, day, and year of your birth.

For example, Sophie was born on July 4, 1988. So you add 7 (July is the seventh month in the year) to 4 (the day) and 1988 (the year). 7 + 4 + 1988 = 1999.

Now add 1 + 9 + 9 + 9 = 28.

If your total is bigger than 22, as Sophie's is, add the two numbers again: 2 + 8 =10. If the number is still larger than 22, keep doing this until your number is less than 22. Then find the Major Arcana card that matches your number. You may notice that The Fool has number 0 and is the first card in the Tarot pack. However, for this exercise The Fool becomes number 22.

Finding Your Personality Card

Your personality card shows how your soul is being expressed in your behavior, actions, thoughts, and feelings. It is how other people see you. You may find that there is some conflict between what your soul wants and what your personality or ego needs.

To find your personality card, add the numbers of your soul card together. For example, Sophie's 10 becomes 1 + 0 = 1. So Sophie's personality card is number 1, The Magician.

If the number of your soul card was a single digit, your personality and soul cards are the same. It's very likely that you don't feel conflicted by what you feel and what you do.

Finding Your Year Card

The card for your year indicates the issues or lessons of that particular year. It will also suggest areas of difficulty, and ways to deal with them.

Before you begin, you need to remember that we are finding out what your card for the present year is. The new year only starts *after* your birthday. So if the date is February 2, 2004, and your birthday isn't until March 2, you are still in a 2003 cycle.

Now add together the day and month of your birth and your present year. For example, Simon's birthday is July 29 and today's date is January 30, 2003. So he adds 7 + 29 + 2002 = 2038. If the date had been August 16, 2003, he would have added 8 + 16 + 2003 =2027.

Now add the digits of the number you get. For example, 2 + 0 + 2 + 7 = 11. The card for the present year is number 11, Justice. If the number is larger than 22, add the digits for that number together to arrive at the number of your year card.

The Card for Today

To find out the general card for today, or any day, add the day, month, and year together. For example July 21, 2003: 7 + 29 + 2003 = 2039. Add the numbers together: 2 + 0 +3 + 9 = 14. The card for that date is Temperance. The card for the day indicates the general mood of the day. For example, The Moon could indicate a quiet, reflective day, while The Chariot suggests a brash and busy one.

Your Personal Card for Today

This card will suggest the personal issues or experiences during the day ahead. Add the month, day, and year of your birth. Then add the current day, month, and year. For example, if your birthday is April 12, 1992, and today's date is May 10, 2003:

4 + 12 + 1992= 2008
5 + 10 + 2003= 2018

Then add the two figures together: 2008 + 2018 = 4026. Reduce the final number. 4 + 0 + 2 + 6 = 12. Your personal card for today is The Hanged Man.

Key Dates

It is intriguing to think about dates in the past and see how the Tarot connects both with your history and that of the world. On September 11, 2001, the Twin Towers of the World Trade Center in New York were attacked, and the world changed. Adding the numbers of the day, month, and year (9 + 11 + 2001) gives us 2021. 2 + 0 + 2 + 1 = 5, the number for The Hierophant. What will immediately strike you is that the Hierophant sits between twin pillars. The Hierophant is no more negative than any other card, but like all the cards it has a negative side. It is the card of authority, morality, and intense religious devotion, but it is also the card of confusion, bewilderment, and disorder—a crisis of faith, combined with people taking the law into their own hands with disastrous consequences.

Your Card for the Week or Month

Using the same technique, you can also find cards associated with certain weeks or months. This could be useful when planning ahead or reflecting on past events.

To figure out the card for a particular week in any year of your choice, find a calendar that can tell you what the week is in the year, and then add it to the number of the year. For example, you have exams in the second week of June in 2003. This is week number 24 added to the year 2003 = 2027. 2 + 0 + 2 + 7 = 11, which is Justice.

To figure out the card for a particular month in the year, add together the month and the year number. For example, for March 2004, add 3 (the number of the month) to 2004, and you get a total of 2007. Add 2 + 0 + 0 + 7, and you get 9. The card is The Hermit.

These techniques can be very useful when you want to choose a date for a special occasion. You may want to plan a party for a day that corresponds with The Sun, or a meeting with your boyfriend or girlfriend on a day that corresponds with The Lovers. Remember, though, that the most important thing is to schedule days and times that suit your friends and family. Don't let the cards get in the way of practicality. If you can't get a day, week, or month that matches the card that you want, it's no big deal; you can always carry the spirit of the card in your heart instead.

10 The Minor Arcana

> ✷ Together, and in union with the archetypal Major cards, they [Minor Arcana] draw us into an even wider knowledge of the changing wonder of life.
>
> —Rachel Pollack, *Seventy-Eight Degrees of Wisdom*

Despite its name, the Minor Arcana, consisting of fifty-six cards, is not less important than the Major. It is best to think of these cards as explanations. They suggest or explain ways for you to approach your life so that it can be a more interesting and fulfilling one.

The four suits of the Tarot's Minor Arcana are traditionally called Wands, Cups, Swords, and Pentacles (or coins). Each suit has cards from ace (or 1) to 10, plus four Court cards—the Page, the Knight, the Queen, and the King. If it helps, you can link the Minor Arcana cards to things that are familiar to you, such as the four suits of your standard playing cards, or the four elements of nature and the signs of the Zodiac—fire, water, earth, and air.

Wands = clubs = fire = signs of Aries, Leo, and Sagittarius

Cups = hearts = water = signs of Cancer, Scorpio, and Pisces

Swords = spades = air = signs of Gemini, Libra, and Aquarius

Pentacles = diamonds = earth = signs of Taurus, Virgo, and Capricorn

Each of the suits of the Minor Arcana is associated with certain areas of your life.

- The suit of Wands suggests energy, ambition, hard work, travel, action, inspiration, and enthusiasm.
- The suit of Cups represents emotions that are connected with love, personal relationships, deep feelings, and creativity.
- The suit of Swords is connected to mental strength, power, action, courage, and overcoming obstacles.
- The suit of Pentacles discusses practical or material things, like health, money, looks, and work.

We'll take a look through the numbered cards of each suit first, and explore the Court cards—Page, Knight, Queen and King—in the next chapter. We'll start with the suit of Wands.

THE SUIT OF WANDS

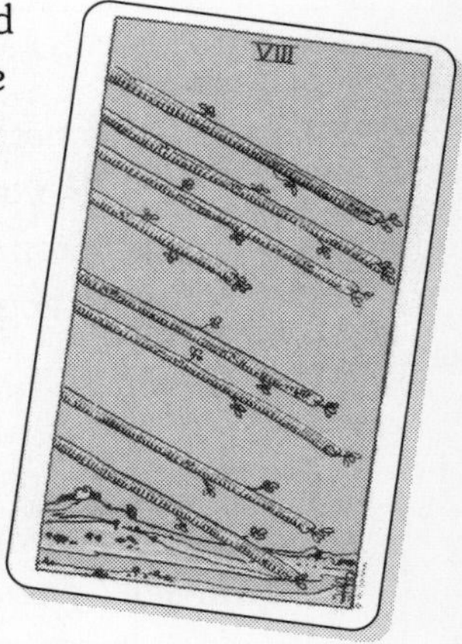

The suit of Wands is associated with fire, action, and energy. Fire is a powerful symbol. It stands for the vital life essence that keeps us alive. If we didn't burn fuel in our stomachs, we would die. Fire symbolizes warmth, and because it rises and leaps forward it stands for optimism, confidence, movement, hope, and the sheer joy of living. The Wands are about positive thinking and believing you can do or be anything you want.

ACE OF WANDS

A hand can be seen coming out of the clouds holding a wand, symbolic of inspiration and energy. The wand is bursting with life and is about to be planted in the earth, because ideas need to be grounded in reality in order to succeed. The wand may also remind you of a pointing finger, suggesting the value of paying attention and thinking carefully about what you say and do.

Questions to ask yourself if you draw the Ace of Wands:

- What are you getting fired up about?
- Are you being offered a new opportunity?
- Is something getting out of hand?
- Are you starting a new project and willing to put in the hard work to achieve your goals?
- Do you feel terrific?

Friends

UPSIDE: The start of a new friendship or a plan that you can work on together with your friends.

DOWNSIDE: Stop badmouthing your friends. Nobody trusts someone who gossips about others behind their back.

School

UPSIDE: An excellent time to get motivated about your schoolwork and start a new project that will raise your academic profile.

DOWNSIDE: There have been too many false starts and too many uncompleted projects. Try and get some focus back.

Dating

UPSIDE: A new romance is, or could soon be, blossoming.

DOWNSIDE: Contain that fiery sexual appetite. It could destroy your chances of a deep and meaningful relationship.

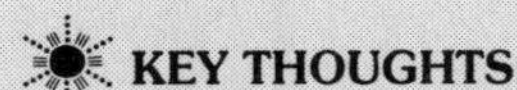 **KEY THOUGHTS:**

Believe in yourself and take action to reach your goals. Don't let fear hold you back. Overcome your fears by learning to believe in yourself more.

Family

UPSIDE: An excellent time to start a new project with other family members—for example, redecorating, or spring cleaning.

DOWNSIDE: You are rushing around and not sharing your experiences with the rest of the family. Try to set aside regular time to talk—really talk—to your family.

Interests

UPSIDE: A new interest will transform your social life. You may be volunteering to tutor someone, or you could be spending time inventing a timesaving device.

DOWNSIDE: Start to focus on one or two things. Too much activity and too many new starts will lead to undirected energy that burns itself out.

Health/Looks

UPSIDE: You love life and life loves you. No worries here.

DOWNSIDE: Keep a sense of humility so that you don't overwhelm people.

Money

UPSIDE: You are full of moneymaking ideas, and your sense of optimism will bring financial reward.

DOWNSIDE: Your financial resources are limited due to poor money management.

30-SECOND READING

Andy has a problem with body odor. Sometimes it's so bad he feels embarrassed to go out. The Ace of Wands is saying that because he is aware of the situation he can do something about it. In the meantime, he needs to make a fresh start and get out there and enjoy life again. His friends may not have noticed his problem, and if they did, because they knew he was doing something about it, it would not affect the way they feel about him.

TWO OF WANDS

This man holds a world, symbolizing success, in his hand. You will notice that he stands in a walled building. He isn't enjoying his success, but stands back and looks out to the horizon. He wants new things to come into his life, but he isn't doing anything about it. It is very easy to just stick with what you know and are good at. For example, you might be the star of a local high school team, but you could do well in that sport standing on your head. It isn't a challenge for you anymore, and you are just sticking with it because it is what you know. This card is about success, but it is also about getting out of your comfort zone (what you know and do well) and trying something new.

Questions to ask yourself if you draw the Two of Wands:

- Are you bored?
- Is life a little too easy?
- What are you longing for?
- Are you feeling restless?
- What are you waiting for?

Friends

UPSIDE: You and your friends are about to do a bit of traveling together (even if it is just going downtown for the afternoon).

DOWNSIDE: You feel very restless at the moment. Don't blame your friends. It's up to you to bring some excitement into your life.

KEY THOUGHTS:
Take the initiative and realize a goal or ambition. The time has come for you to set targets and take action to reach those targets. Face your fears. Every time you do something you thought you couldn't, your confidence grows. Step out of that comfort zone. Set new challenges, however small, and you'll grow in confidence and happiness.

School

UPSIDE: Anything that involves geography or analytical thinking is going well at the moment.

DOWNSIDE: Find out why you feel so dissatisfied at school. Are you being challenged? Are you studying the right subjects?

Dating

UPSIDE: You are sensible beyond your years and need a partner who is as mature as you are.

DOWNSIDE: Do you know what you want? Are you sure? Make up your mind before someone—and that could be you—really gets hurt.

Family

UPSIDE: Life at home is like a comforting refuge from the world.

DOWNSIDE: Don't lead such a sheltered life that you can't make that move to independence when the time comes for you to spread your wings.

Interests

UPSIDE: Opportunities to indulge your growing interest in travel are coming up.

DOWNSIDE: You can't concentrate on anything for long and are watching far too much TV. Try reading a good book instead.

Health/Looks

UPSIDE: You may have felt unattractive in the recent past, but your confidence has returned and you are ready to wow the world.

DOWNSIDE: Insecurity about your looks leaves you isolated and alone.

Money

UPSIDE: You will soon be less restricted financially and will enjoy the freedom this gives you.

DOWNSIDE: Don't get so fixated on saving or earning money that you forget to have fun with it.

30-SECOND READING

It is summertime, and Suzy is bored. She is hanging around the house, getting on everybody's nerves. If something exciting does not happen soon, she will scream. The Two of Wands is saying that she needs to make something happen rather than sitting around waiting for it to happen to her. A summer camp is coming up soon, and she should ask her parents if she can go. It would be just what she needs right now.

THREE OF WANDS

A man is standing on solid ground looking out to sea. The solid ground represents his achievements, and the ships on the horizon represent his ideas. His ships, or plans, have just been launched, and now is the time to see if things are going to work out. He is a solitary figure and probably would feel a lot happier if he asked for assistance from other people somewhere along the line. Generally, the Three of Wands means success, but it can also mean feeling frustrated or blocked in your ideas, or spending too much time talking about ideas and not enough time actually carrying them out.

Questions to ask yourself if you draw the Three of Wands:

- Are you launching a new idea or project?
- Too much talking and not enough doing?
- Do you need to ask someone for help or advice?
- Do you have the courage of your convictions? Will you see things through?
- Are you waiting for something or someone?

Friends

UPSIDE: You can still look for new friends while maintaining commitment to existing friendships. It doesn't have to be one or the other.
DOWNSIDE: Don't be too proud to ask for help, advice, or just a long talk. Sharing is a sign of strength, not weakness.

School

UPSIDE: Rome wasn't built in a day. Success in exams requires steady, regular work and self-discipline.
DOWNSIDE: There are no shortcuts to exam success. Don't even think about cheating.

Dating

UPSIDE: You are prepared to work hard at an important relationship. Your determination will yield positive results.
DOWNSIDE: Are you putting any effort into your relationship? If you aren't, think about why you aren't and make a decision. If you can't make your partner happy, let your partner go so he or she can find happiness with someone else.

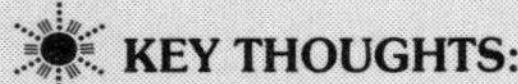

KEY THOUGHTS:
Think positive. A positive attitude will help create positive results. Visualize yourself getting what you want or being where you want to be. Keep focusing on your goal, and work toward it. This increase of focus and energy will make you far more likely to achieve what you want.

Family

UPSIDE: Your family thinks of you as an old soul. Your wisdom and sound judgment are amazing.

DOWNSIDE: Stop being so detached from your family. They could benefit from your insight and feedback.

Interests

UPSIDE: You might start showing an interest in politics or law.

DOWNSIDE: Are you interested in anything at the moment? Why are you letting boredom take up so much of your time?

Health/Looks

UPSIDE: You are at peace with yourself, and this manifests in a confidence and maturity beyond your years.

DOWNSIDE: You aren't the unpopular kid in the class anymore. Stop putting yourself down. You really are cool.

Money

UPSIDE: Your hard work is paying off. You can enjoy your success and keep an eye out for future opportunity.

DOWNSIDE: There is too much schoolwork for you to catch up on, and you simply haven't got time to find ways to earn extra cash.

30-SECOND READING
Aaron is interested in the Tarot and spends a lot of time working with Tarot cards. The Three of Wands is saying that Aaron needs to find things that can challenge him mentally and physically. It is good that he is enjoying the Tarot, but there is a whole world out there for him to explore as well.

FOUR OF WANDS

The Four of Wands is about happiness and teamwork. The dancing couple have been in a walled environment (somewhere unhappy or restrictive) but have found a way out and are now happy and free. The fact that they are dancing shows that nothing can be done in isolation. We all need to work together and compromise when necessary to achieve a good end result.

Questions to ask yourself if you draw the Four of Wands:

- Are you feeling happy?
- Are you counting your blessings?
- Are you celebrating?
- How are you helping to make this a better world?
- What group have you joined or recently left?

Friends

UPSIDE: Your friends are good for you, and you are good for them.

DOWNSIDE: You don't always appreciate your friends. Let them know how important they are to you before it is too late.

School

UPSIDE: You are, or soon will be, celebrating a team victory.

DOWNSIDE: Don't be miserable about school or college rituals, like morning meetings. They help create a sense of community spirit.

Dating

UPSIDE: A very special occasion or anniversary is coming up.

DOWNSIDE: Don't have such a pessimistic view about weddings. They are a wonderful celebration of love, joy, and togetherness. Yes, many marriages fail, but don't forget there also are many that last.

Family

UPSIDE: A happy time for you and your family. Treasure these moments. They will be a source of inspiration and strength in the years ahead.

DOWNSIDE: Don't sit on the sidelines and withdraw from family gatherings. Take part and enjoy.

KEY THOUGHTS:

Let your spirit and courage carry you, and the people you care about, from a difficult situation into a happier one. Keep tackling new things, and watch your confidence grow as success comes more easily.

Interests

UPSIDE: Lots of invitations to events and parties are coming up. Enjoy.

DOWNSIDE: Are you feeling like an outsider? Why aren't you joining in?

Health/Looks

UPSIDE: You may soon take someone's advice and make changes in your personal style. These changes will be positive ones, and you will have lots of fun with your new look.

DOWNSIDE: Slavishly following the latest fashion trends doesn't say you are fashionable; it just says you lack imagination.

Money

UPSIDE: Money has come your way, or will come soon if you are willing to put in the effort.

DOWNSIDE: Stop focusing on what you don't have, and appreciate what you do have.

30-SECOND READING

Pia is trying to finish an important literature assignment. She does not really understand it and isn't pleased with what she has done. The Four of Wands is saying that success comes down to teamwork. This team includes her friends, teachers, and parents. If she asks all of them for help, she will make great progress.

FIVE OF WANDS

In the Five of Wands card we see five men fighting each other, but the conflict isn't an intense one. They are hitting each other lightly, almost as if they are play-fighting. This suggests that life is a game and we need a certain amount of challenge to make us feel alive. Sometimes this card is about inner conflict rather than conflict in the outside world. You'll see that the figures all face in different directions, suggesting differing opinions or conflicting interests and the need for someone to impose order.

Questions to ask yourself if you draw the Five of Wands:

- Are you involved in a dispute?
- Is there something you just aren't sure about?
- What needs to be organized?
- Are you enjoying healthy competition?
- Why can't you reach a compromise?

Friends

UPSIDE: Lots of great conversations at the moment. You have lots to think about.

DOWNSIDE: A lot of disagreement at the moment among your friends. A compromise needs to be found before too much damage is done and someone really gets hurt.

School

UPSIDE: This is an excellent time to join a debating society or to express your ideas to those in authority.

DOWNSIDE: Petty conflicts and tensions among your classmates are keeping you from concentrating. Find a way out, so you can focus on learning.

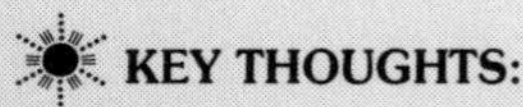

KEY THOUGHTS: Compete for the sheer joy of it. Life isn't about winning or losing; it is about living.

Dating

UPSIDE: Difference of opinion is healthy. In the long run it will strengthen and build any relationship.

DOWNSIDE: If you are in a relationship, you are arguing way too much and hurting each other in the process. Find some middle ground.

Family

UPSIDE: Listening to the different opinions and viewpoints of family members will help you decide what is important to you.

DOWNSIDE: Family conflicts are wearing everybody down. Take some time out to have fun with your friends.

Interests

UPSIDE: Are you channeling your aggressive energy into contact sports? If you aren't, get a punching bag.

DOWNSIDE: Turn the television off when talk shows are on, and find something else to fill your time.

Health/Looks

UPSIDE: You are blessed with a healthy constitution.

DOWNSIDE: If you want to dress a certain way and your parents and/or school are against it, you need to learn to compromise. Fight the battles that are worth fighting, not those that aren't. Your relationship with your parents and your progress at school is far more important than a nose ring or pink hair rinse.

Money

UPSIDE: It's a struggle for you to make ends meet, but you enjoy the challenge.

DOWNSIDE: Sometimes you need to set aside personal gain for the benefit of the group.

30-SECOND READING

Jocelyn is arguing with her parents all the time. This card suggests that the tension at home is wearing down both Jocelyn and her parents. She needs to back off and find another way to get her point across. She also needs to recognize that her parents have an opinion. Once she can start to see her parents' point of view as well as her own, she can work with her parents toward a compromise.

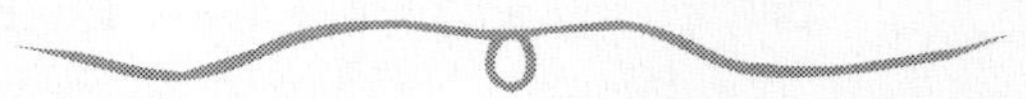

SIX OF WANDS

The Six of Wands is a card of victory. The hero is surrounded by his followers and they are cheering him on. He has not yet reached his goal, but he is about to. The fact that he assumes he is going to reach his goal tells us that he is a very positive, upbeat person. He also recognizes that he needs the support of other people to reach his goal. He doesn't want anyone to turn on him and block his way when he is so close to victory.

Questions to ask yourself if you draw the Six of Wands:

- Is everyone rallying around you?
- What victory are you enjoying?
- Are you recognizing the needs of those around you?
- Are you feeling positive?
- Are you feeling proud?

Friends

UPSIDE: You treat your friends with respect, and they love you for it.
DOWNSIDE: Are there people you are neglecting?

School

UPSIDE: You are assuming a number of positions of responsibility at school. They are an excellent preparation for adult life.
DOWNSIDE: You are doing your best to undermine peers who are trying really hard to do well at school. Stop doing this. It reflects badly on you.

Dating

UPSIDE: You are almost there. The boy or girl of your dreams is about to recognize what a terrific person you are.
DOWNSIDE: Stop putting yourself down. Other people would love to get to know you. Give yourself a chance.

Family

UPSIDE: You and your family make a great team.
DOWNSIDE: Stop passing judgment at home. You are no better than anyone else, just different.

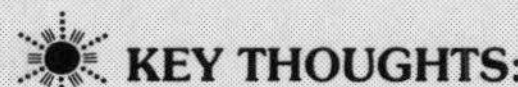

KEY THOUGHTS: Acknowledge feelings of fear and overcome them by learning to believe in yourself. Victory will certainly be yours if you keep believing in yourself and work with others to achieve your goal.

Interests

UPSIDE: You are about to realize a lifelong dream or ambition. This time you will compete and win.
DOWNSIDE: Lack of self-belief keeps you from competing at your best.

Health/Looks

UPSIDE: You feel great about yourself, and you look great, too.
DOWNSIDE: Are you feeling inferior to other people? It's time to work on your self-confidence.

Money

UPSIDE: Keep working hard. You will soon have the financial rewards you deserve.
DOWNSIDE: Money seems to slip through your fingers. You need to learn how to manage money.

30-SECOND READING

Louise is quite nervous. Commencement is coming up, and she knows she has won a number of awards. She is half looking forward to it and half wondering if she will make a fool of herself. She worries that her friends will think she is a Goody Two-Shoes. This card is telling her to relax and just enjoy. If her friends put her down, it is just because they are jealous. She will remember this day for a long time, and has certainly earned all the praise.

SEVEN OF WANDS

A man on a cliff uses his wand to defend himself from six others below. You will notice that the man is on raised ground, suggesting that he has risen above his problems and is enjoying the exhilaration and excitement of the conflict. He has also separated himself from peer pressure. This guy is doing his own thing. The Seven of Wands teaches us the importance of strategy or planning. If he tries to attack all six at once he will fail. He needs to focus on one problem at a time to knock out the opposition.

Questions to ask yourself if you draw the Seven of Wands:

- What do you feel you have risen above?
- Are you staying on top of things?
- Are you holding your own or do you need help?
- Are you confronting some opposition?
- Are you standing up for your beliefs?

Friends

UPSIDE: You had disagreements with your friends but have resolved them.

DOWNSIDE: Your friends' problems are starting to overwhelm you. Remember, you are not responsible for your friends, and you can't live their lives for them.

School

UPSIDE: You are prepared to stand up for what you believe in and will earn respect from your peers and teachers alike.

DOWNSIDE: Problems at school are threatening to overwhelm you. Seek help now.

Dating

UPSIDE: Just because everybody else has a date doesn't mean you have to have one. You will date when you meet the person who is right for you.

DOWNSIDE: You may feel that your partner or someone you like is trying to undermine you. Stand up to them.

KEY THOUGHTS:

Decide on a clear course of action, and you will overcome any anxieties and problems you may be facing. Change your language. Keep your language positive; it reflects your thoughts and actions. Don't think "problem"; think "challenge." Then enjoy meeting that challenge.

Family

UPSIDE: Your family might have problems, but you can work together to resolve them.

DOWNSIDE: Conflicting interests are causing problems within your family. Don't let them overwhelm you. Find ways to rise above the tension.

Interests

UPSIDE: You have the gift of the gab. You could be a great salesperson, politician, or lawyer.

DOWNSIDE: You aren't willing to try new things. Think about why you are being so defensive.

Health/Looks

UPSIDE: You enjoy creating new styles and looking different from your peers. You're a true individual.

DOWNSIDE: Don't let other people tell you how to look and feel. Decide for yourself.

Money

UPSIDE: You are good at coming up with moneymaking schemes and acting upon them.

DOWNSIDE: Too much talk and too little action means that money won't be coming your way.

30-SECOND READING

Elsa feels down. Everything is going wrong at the moment at school, at home, and with her boyfriend. She wants to know what she can do. This card is telling her that she should tackle one thing at a time in her life. She should also stop thinking of her life as a series of problems; instead, she should see it as a series of challenges. "Problems" make it sound as if things can't be fixed. "Challenges," on the other hand, encourage you to search for a solution.

EIGHT OF WANDS

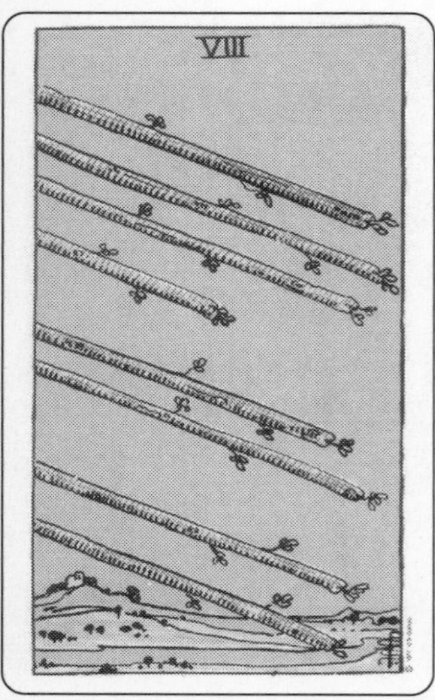

The Eight of Wands is a card of possibilities. There are many directions you could be headed in. However, if you don't make a decision about where you want to go, results will be disappointing or nonexistent. The Wands can be seen as falling to earth or rising from it. You could be heading toward something or leaving something behind. You will need to act in a detached, calm way if you are to achieve the results you want. Don't make any hasty decisions, as you will regret them later.

Questions to ask yourself if you draw the Eight of Wands:

- Where are you off to?
- Where are you coming from?

- Are you always on the go?
- Are you full of new ideas?
- Is everything up in the air?

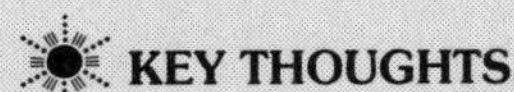

KEY THOUGHTS:

Things are moving quickly, and you have boundless energy and enthusiasm. Make a decision about which direction to head in. You have the ability, but sometimes lack the self-belief.

Friends

UPSIDE: Your energy level is so high at the moment that your friends can hardly keep up. Slow down a little.

DOWNSIDE: Friendship isn't about the phone constantly ringing, or party invitations. Better to have one or two good friends than lots of people you don't really know well.

School

UPSIDE: Your studies are going in a new and exciting direction.

DOWNSIDE: Your studies are all up in the air at the moment. Better planning is needed.

Dating

UPSIDE: You are so much in love, it almost hurts.

DOWNSIDE: Don't start dating two or more people. It's hurtful and dishonest and just exhausting!

Family

UPSIDE: Your family is a busy one, and there is never a dull moment.

DOWNSIDE: Stop being so fidgety, impatient, and uneasy at home. These people love you. You haven't got anything to prove.

Interests

UPSIDE: You have so many interests that there aren't enough hours in the day.

DOWNSIDE: Slow down a little. You are moving too fast, and this could be dangerous.

Health/Looks

UPSIDE: You always keep up with the latest trends and are an inspiration to your friends.
DOWNSIDE: You are doing too much, and this is affecting your health. Slow down.

Money

UPSIDE: You are excited about a new moneymaking idea. If you think things through carefully, it should all work out fine.
DOWNSIDE: Money is important, but if you are working too many hours you will just end up exhausted and unhappy.

30-SECOND READING

John isn't sure whether to go to college or get a job right away. The Eight of Wands is saying that he is the kind of person who will do well whatever he decides, but if he takes the time to really think things through, he will see that college will increase his chances of getting more satisfying and better-paid work.

NINE OF WANDS

In the Nine of Wands we see a warrior-like man with a bandage around his head—indicating that he been in a battle—standing apart from the other Wands. The look on his face suggests that he is alert to potential danger. Only time will tell if his watchful attitude to life is justified or not. Is he alert or is he paranoid? Take a look at the picture and see what you think. Expect the unexpected if you get this card. Beware of things going on around you that you may not be aware of yet. Watch for opportunities, and be certain of your facts before acting.

Questions to ask yourself if you draw the Nine of Wands:

- Who or what are you suspicious of?
- Are you standing your ground?
- Do you feel you need to defend yourself?
- Do you feel exhausted because you are always on the alert?
- Do you feel you can trust other people?

Friends

UPSIDE: You are a great support to your friends through good times and bad times.
DOWNSIDE: You don't trust your friends and feel you need to keep your defenses up all the time.

School

UPSIDE: You are one of those people who "gets" what school is all about. You understand that without an education, your chances in life are limited.
DOWNSIDE: You are one of those people who doesn't "get" it. Stop rebelling and wasting time.

Dating

UPSIDE: Although you may feel alone right now, use this time to think about what is important to you in a relationship so that when you do meet the boy or girl of your dreams, you won't hesitate to act.
DOWNSIDE: Jealousy and mistrust in a relationship will eventually destroy it.

Family

UPSIDE: The support of your family helps you through difficult times. Your family is like your rock, and with them behind you, you feel you can face anything.

DOWNSIDE: Getting the support you need from your family won't always be easy.

KEY THOUGHTS: Self-image is largely formed by the feedback we get from other people. Gaining awareness is the first step. It's often the case that other people don't realize what they are doing. If you think you can't do something, step back and look at why you think this. Approach it differently and positively, and you'll make the breakthrough.

Interests

UPSIDE: Your self-confidence is so high right now you could tackle just about anything.

DOWNSIDE: Don't let fear keep you from doing things you really want to do.

Health/Looks

UPSIDE: You take care of your health and are putting your body image problems firmly in the past.

DOWNSIDE: You are getting too anxious about your health and your appearance.

Money

UPSIDE: You are prepared to work long and hard to improve your finances. Your efforts will not go unrewarded.

DOWNSIDE: Do you feel overwhelmed right now? Do you worry that you will never be able to take care of yourself financially? Ask for help and advice.

30-SECOND READING

Tom doesn't think he is any good at math. His teacher has separated the class into the mathematicians and the non-mathematicians. The mathematicians make fun of him when he struggles with his work. This card is saying that instead of thinking he has no ability, Tom should think of other reasons for his lack of ability. Perhaps bad teaching methods have something to do with it?

TEN OF WANDS

The figure in the card is carrying a whole stack of heavy wands. He struggles with the load, and his back is bent over. Wands are symbols of taking on responsibility and going for new challenges. Sometimes we take on too many responsibilities and end up exhausted. Are you the kind of person who feels responsible for the problems of everyone? Are you doing your friends' homework for them? Have you joined lots of after-school clubs? Do you have a Saturday job? Are you looking after a kid brother or sister? Do you feel you are running hard but getting nowhere?

Questions to ask yourself if you draw the Ten of Wands:

- What is weighing you down?
- What have you decided to do no matter what?
- Why don't you ask for help?
- Is your burden heavy or light?
- Have you taken on too much?

Friends

UPSIDE: You are helping your friends a lot right now, and this makes you—and them—feel good.
DOWNSIDE: Don't forget that you need someone to listen to you, too.

School

UPSIDE: You have to set priorities. You can't be good at everything. Your energy is commendable, but there are only so many hours in the day.
DOWNSIDE: Things are getting overwhelming. Ask for help.

Dating

UPSIDE: It's time to decide whom you are interested in. You can only go out with one person at a time.

DOWNSIDE: A romance or crush could come to an abrupt end. This is your chance to move forward.

KEY THOUGHTS:

You may feel like you're at a breaking point with all the pressures that are on your shoulders—pressures to be cool, to do well at school, get into college, get a job, please your parents, please your teachers, and so on. Or perhaps you want to show the world that you don't care, when in fact you care very much. Both these responses stem from fear. Fear can hold you back, stop you, make you take on too many commitments. And fear stems from lack of belief in your abilities. What a shame! If only you knew how much you are capable of!

Family

UPSIDE: Consider lessening the load of responsibilities your family is placing upon you.

DOWNSIDE: Family tensions are dangerously close to disrupting your life. Seek help and advice outside the family.

Interests

UPSIDE: What have you set your mind on doing, no matter what?

DOWNSIDE: Are you being overly ambitious and a little selfish in your aims?

Health/Looks

UPSIDE: You have worked hard to improve your body image. Don't give up now; you are almost there.

DOWNSIDE: You are tempted to quit exercising and eating healthfully. Don't. You will regret it.

Money

UPSIDE: Losses are inevitable, but they can be minimized if you tread carefully.

DOWNSIDE: You may feel trapped in a work situation or by debt.

30-SECOND READING

Dustin wants to give his friend a surprise birthday party. He is worried about coming up with good ideas for the party. This card is warning Dustin that there is a danger that he will get so caught up in organizing this party and worrying about what will happen that he won't be able to enjoy it. He needs to concentrate on what is important here—having a party that's fun for everyone, including him.

THE SUIT OF CUPS

Cups are associated with water, which signifies who you are—your inner being. The cards in this suit represent your feelings, and are associated with anything emotional, from the love you feel for someone to your hopes and dreams for the future. Your relationships with others are covered by the suit of Cups, but these cards also stress the importance of your relationship with yourself.

ACE OF CUPS

Ace of Cups is a card of happiness and love. The dove represents the Holy Spirit, or the goodness in all of us, and the cup is the Holy Grail. Legend has it that if the cup of the Holy Grail could be found, happiness and joy would come to the kingdom of King Arthur. The Knights of the Round Table never found the cup, but in this card the heavens are giving it to you. All you have to do is seize the moment; reach out and take it.

Questions to ask yourself if you draw the Ace of Cups:

- Is a dream about to be fulfilled?
- Is your heart opening up to yourself or someone else?
- Have you found your heart's desire?
- Do you feel empty?
- Does love make your world go round?

Friends

UPSIDE: Everyone wants to be with someone as upbeat and happy as you.

DOWNSIDE: A false friend. Jealousy is poisoning a friendship—try to step back from it.

School

UPSIDE: A teacher is giving you information that could fulfill a long-held dream.

DOWNSIDE: You are not being challenged at school. Ask your teachers to help you find ways to achieve your potential.

Dating

UPSIDE: Things look promising for a new relationship. Love is in the air, and all the emotions and traumas associated with love, whether being in love or falling in love, are present, too.

DOWNSIDE: The feelings you have for someone are unlikely to be returned.

Family

UPSIDE: The birth of a child, an engagement, or a new relationship or marriage is in the cards for someone in your family.

DOWNSIDE: Unwelcome changes in family routine are likely.

Interests

UPSIDE: You may be drawn to some kind of counseling, advising, or even psychic work—anything that encourages people to talk about the way they feel.

DOWNSIDE: You may find yourself falling into a despondent mood because you don't have enough interests outside school and home.

Health/Looks

UPSIDE: You are a happy, healthy person, at peace with the way you look.

DOWNSIDE: Stop being so critical about your appearance. Even supermodels have bad hair days.

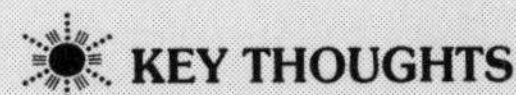

Dream about your goals. Imagine a detailed image of your success and use that image to focus and motivate you. Then you can start to live your dreams.

Money

UPSIDE: This is the card of opportunity. You will find a way to bring in extra cash.

DOWNSIDE: You may have overspent recently. It will take a while before you pay back your debts.

30-SECOND READING

Patsy is excited. Her favorite pop group will be playing in a local stadium. She has a massive crush on the lead singer. This card says that there is opportunity for her to learn about love at her school. She shouldn't let her crush keep her from living her life to the fullest. There are plenty of boys interested in her. All she needs to do is give them a chance to get to know her.

TWO OF CUPS

A young man and a young woman are getting acquainted in the Two of Cups. It suggests the start of a new relationship or the celebration of an existing one. You will notice a winged lion at the top, symbolizing sexuality and healing. A loving relationship can be very healing. But the card may also suggest self-love and the merging of the traditionally masculine (representing action) and feminine (representing emotion). It is only when you can unite what you do with what you feel that you can feel truly fulfilled.

Questions to ask yourself if you draw the Two of Cups:

- Is this your first serious relationship?
- Are you getting more in touch with your feelings?
- What are you sharing?
- Do you love yourself enough?
- Are you compromising something?

Friends

UPSIDE: A close friend is very different from you, but you learn much from each other.

DOWNSIDE: A friendship is in trouble because you are not taking the time to listen to what your friend is trying to tell you.

School

UPSIDE: Two very different subjects are interesting to you at the moment.

DOWNSIDE: You are finding school particularly difficult right now. Ask for help, and you will get it.

Dating

UPSIDE: It looks as though you are or will soon be in a fulfilling and happy relationship.

DOWNSIDE: You are fearing or experiencing a broken relationship. There could be misunderstandings, and conflicting aims and desires. Guard against someone who appears excessively charming. They are not what they seem.

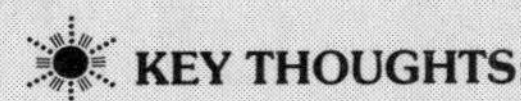

KEY THOUGHTS: Summon up your courage, and share your thoughts and feelings with people you trust. By sharing your feelings you learn to lighten up and not take yourself so seriously.

Family

UPSIDE: You come from a caring, sharing, and loving family.

DOWNSIDE: You need to learn to compromise more.

Interests

UPSIDE: Your interests tend to revolve around your loved ones. It might be a good idea to broaden your horizons. Have you thought about music, dance, or the arts?

DOWNSIDE: Someone could take advantage of your sensitive, reflective, and altruistic nature. Be careful.

Health/Looks

UPSIDE: You have sex appeal and know how to turn on the charm when you want to.

DOWNSIDE: A poor body image is holding you back.

Money

UPSIDE: You may find that problems with colleagues at work, or disagreements about money at home, start to fade.

DOWNSIDE: You have financial worries due to poor money management.

30-SECOND READING

Rinka thinks all her friends are more popular, more attractive, more clever, and so on. She doesn't feel at all confident about herself and wants to lose lots of weight. The card is saying that she is fine just as she is and should stop comparing herself to other people. She needs to work on her self-esteem, and if she feels she needs help, she should talk to someone she can trust.

THREE OF CUPS

The Three of Cups is the card of friendship and celebration. You will notice that the three women have their arms entwined. They are so closely involved with one another that they seem to be one. Working together as a group can often be more powerful than trying to do something as an individual. A happy social life is indicated by this card.

Questions to ask yourself if you draw the Three of Cups:

- Are you enjoying love or companionship with friends and family?
- What experience are you sharing?
- Do you feel like celebrating?
- Are you working toward a common goal?
- Are you outgrowing certain friendships?

KEY THOUGHTS:
A difficult situation is about to end, and problems will be resolved. As you work through your difficulties you will gain more knowledge about yourself. Self-knowledge helps you build confidence and gain control of your life.

Friends

UPSIDE: Good times ahead. Perhaps a party or get-together is planned.
DOWNSIDE: It is time to seek out new friends. You no longer have much in common with your old friends.

School

UPSIDE: Team activities will not only be great learning opportunities, they will also be a lot of fun.
DOWNSIDE: You are so involved with your friends that you are neglecting your learning.

Dating

UPSIDE: Whether or not you are in a relationship, you are a happy person.
DOWNSIDE: You could find yourself the target of someone's unwelcome attentions.

Family

UPSIDE: A family celebration is coming up. It will be a joyful occasion.
DOWNSIDE: Lack of communication at home is causing problems.

Interests

UPSIDE: You are using your spare time to help other people, and this brings a great deal of happiness to you and to them.
DOWNSIDE: Time to look around for some new interests to challenge you. Have you thought about volunteer work?

Health/Looks

UPSIDE: If you have been feeling ill recently, you should be feeling better now.
DOWNSIDE: Watch out for unhealthy eating and drinking patterns.

Money

UPSIDE: You may soon find yourself in a healthier financial situation, if you haven't already.

DOWNSIDE: It's tough not having enough money, but don't let it get you down. The situation will improve soon.

30-SECOND READING

Dawn wants to know what she can do to make friends. The cards are suggesting that it won't be long before she is surrounded by friends. She needs to work on her confidence, show an interest in other people, and get involved when she can.

FOUR OF CUPS

The Four of Cups can indicate laziness, but it is more likely to suggest a need for patience and reflection. The three cups at the front of the card have run dry, which suggests that it is no good looking to the past, because the past is gone. Perhaps you have outgrown something or someone, or you could be missing opportunities because your mind is too stuck on the past. A cup is being offered from the sky. This can mean that new possibilities are coming your way if you follow your inner promptings rather than those of others.

Questions to ask yourself if you draw the Four of Cups:

- Should you be waiting for a better offer?
- What are you waiting for?
- Do you like what you are being offered?
- Why are you feeling lazy?
- Is there something or someone you are rejecting?

Friends

UPSIDE: You may be feeling a little left out, unloved, and unwanted by your friends—a good time to think about building new friendships.

DOWNSIDE: You may feel resentful, but try to avoid any confrontation. It isn't worth it.

School

UPSIDE: You are not one to speak up in class, but when you do, your words carry remarkable insight and wisdom.

DOWNSIDE: Too much sitting on the sidelines. Time to get involved.

Dating

UPSIDE: If you are happy in your own company, this is a good time to think about a relationship. If you aren't happy in your own company, the relationship you should be working on is the one with yourself.

DOWNSIDE: Not a great deal of action taking place in this area of your life.

Family

UPSIDE: A solution will be found to something that has been bothering your family for some time.

DOWNSIDE: A lot of resentment and tension at home.

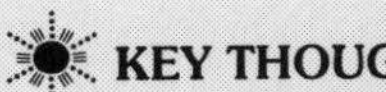

KEY THOUGHTS:

Now is a good time to think about how the mind works and how it is possible to think yourself into success or failure. A new start, new directions, and new hope are on the horizon. Things will turn out better than expected, and this should teach you that optimism sometimes pays.

Interests

UPSIDE: This is a good time to learn new things, join new social groups, and meet new people. You may be drawn toward social work or nursing or politics in the future.

DOWNSIDE: You are making plans but aren't seeing much progress. Use this time to think through things without jeopardizing other projects.

Health/Looks

UPSIDE: Watch your stress levels. Time to recharge your batteries.
DOWNSIDE: Too little activity takes its toll on your health.

Money

UPSIDE: Possibilities abound for making money.
DOWNSIDE: Problems with money cause resentment and tension.

30-SECOND READING

Aaron had such a great time in middle school. He isn't enjoying high school at all, and wishes he could go back in time. This card is telling him that he can't re-create the past. All he can do is concentrate on what is going on in his life right now. In a few years' time, what is going on now will have become his past, and he needs to make sure he has lots of wonderful memories to look back on.

FIVE OF CUPS

The river of sorrow flows in this card, but it is crossed by a bridge, which suggests that the past is moving gently away and a bright new future is on the horizon. The figure in the card wears a black cloak and sobs over the three cups she has spilled. What she doesn't realize is that two cups are still standing. Once she has finished mourning her past, she needs to turn herself around and see the possibilities that await her.

Questions to ask yourself if you draw the Five of Cups:

- What's upsetting you?
- What have you lost?
- What loss can't you come to terms with?
- What are you turning away from?
- Have any plans been disrupted?

Friends

UPSIDE: Any quarrels or splits you may have had are behind you. Good times lie ahead.
DOWNSIDE: You may have lost touch with people, and regret it.

School

UPSIDE: Results at school have been disappointing, but you are learning from your mistakes and doing all you can to correct them.
DOWNSIDE: You may feel like giving up. Don't.

Dating

UPSIDE: Rifts with loved ones will be healed.
DOWNSIDE: A sense of loss remains after a breakup, but your friends will give you the support you need at this difficult time.

Family

UPSIDE: You love your family, but feel the need for more independence.
DOWNSIDE: Anxiety about leaving home may keep you from focusing on the wonderful opportunities that lie ahead.

Interests

UPSIDE: You are ready to move on to new interests and social groups. Have you thought about teaching?

KEY THOUGHTS:

You have grown up with attitudes that lead to set beliefs that you don't question, and some of these beliefs may be limiting you. From now on, every time a negative belief holds you back, replace it with a positive one. That means "I can't" becomes "maybe I could," and "I'm no good" becomes "let's see if I can do this."

DOWNSIDE: Stop being so negative about everything. It isn't uncool to have passion and enthusiasm.

Health/Looks

UPSIDE: You have not taken good care of yourself in the past, but are starting to realize just how important good health is.

DOWNSIDE: Your negative frame of mind is making you look less attractive than you could be.

Money

UPSIDE: You may find yourself with a little extra money, through overtime, an inheritance, or a small prize.

DOWNSIDE: Money is scarce, but you feel rich as friends rally around to support you.

30-SECOND READING

Sarah has been trying for years to make the varsity cheerleading squad, but each time she misses the grade. This card tells her that it is time to let go of this particular dream and try other things. There are lots of opportunities ahead for her, but she must first leave the past behind so she can let the future in.

SIX OF CUPS

The Six of Cups is the card of sweet memories. A dwarf, which represents the past, is seen giving a gift of memories to the future, represented by the child. Sometimes the memories are real, but sometimes they are idealized. Either way, these memories give us a secure feeling, which can help us face current problems. Sometimes, though, a fixation on the past can keep us from enjoying the present. Memories should be enjoyed, but they should not stop you from living in the here and now.

Questions to ask yourself if you draw the Six of Cups:

- Are you living in the past?
- What are your feelings about growing up?
- Do you feel loved and protected?
- Are you clinging to old ideas?
- Who is offering you love, or to whom are you offering love?

Friends

UPSIDE: A friend from the past returns for a brief visit. Enjoy reminiscing about the good old days.

DOWNSIDE: You are focusing too much on the friends you have lost or left behind. It is time to move on and make new friends.

School

UPSIDE: One teacher in particular may be giving you a lot of support and encouragement right now.

DOWNSIDE: Your attitude is making it hard for your teachers to help you. Stop throwing the gift of learning back in their face.

Dating

UPSIDE: Before you jump into a relationship, find out more about your potential partner. What you learn may change your opinion.

DOWNSIDE: Guard against being overly suspicious of your boyfriend or girlfriend.

Family

UPSIDE: You feel loved and protected by your family. This gives you a wonderful sense of security, which helps you face current problems.

DOWNSIDE: Don't let your family be your only source of comfort and security. Allow friends and mentors to help you, too.

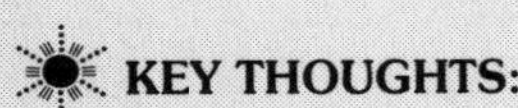

Deep inside you is the small, helpless child you once were, and this helpless child craves love, encouragement, and affection. Very often the one who harms your inner child the most is not someone else, but you—the very one who should be loving and caring. Praise and encourage yourself a little more.

Interests

UPSIDE: You are likely to find a use for skills you have put aside. Creative talents, like music, art, and dance will reappear. You may enjoy working with younger children.

DOWNSIDE: Don't let all that hard work and training go to waste. Put your skills to good use.

Health/Looks

UPSIDE: A great time to update your wardrobe and personal style.

DOWNSIDE: Constantly changing your image could indicate a lack of confidence. Try building up your self-esteem instead of your wardrobe.

Money

UPSIDE: This is a good time for moneymaking opportunities.

DOWNSIDE: You are relying too much on your family for financial support and need to find ways to generate some spare cash of your own.

30-SECOND READING

Rona's boyfriend wants their relationship to become more physical, but she knows this isn't what her parents would want her to do. This card suggests that Rona needs to talk to her

(continued)

parents and decide whether she is ready to look to the future with her boyfriend or respect her parents' wishes. Whatever decision she makes, this card suggests that her family will love and support her.

SEVEN OF CUPS

The seven cups in this picture are filled with visions. We see an array of possibilities that a person can choose in their life, from wealth to adventure to sex to fame and fortune. The main problem with the cups is that the visions are daydreams and aren't grounded in reality and action. Sometimes it is fun to daydream, but this card warns against being unrealistic and foolish.

Questions to ask yourself if you draw the Seven of Cups:

- What are you trying to avoid by living in a fantasyland?
- What are you dreaming about?
- Are you faced with difficult choices?
- Is your head in the clouds?
- Are you wishing for the impossible?

Friends

UPSIDE: You have lots of friends but are feeling the need to bond with just a few.

DOWNSIDE: Many of your friends do not have your best interests at heart. It is time to decide who your real friends are.

School

UPSIDE: Creative writing and anything that involves imagination will go especially well. You may also be enjoying philosophical and religious studies.

DOWNSIDE: You are talking too much about what you want to do. Time to get down to it.

Dating

UPSIDE: You could go out with a number of boys or girls at the moment. Whom will you choose? Make sure you think carefully before you make your decision.

DOWNSIDE: Your head is in the clouds about a certain person or relationship. Time to get real, and see things as they really are.

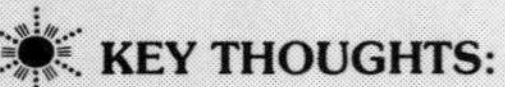

KEY THOUGHTS: Daydreams have their place, but realize that you are living in the real world. If you want your dreams to become reality, you have to set goals, plan how you are going to achieve them, and then get out there and start working toward them.

Family

UPSIDE: Some exciting new plans on the horizon that will involve the whole family, including you.

DOWNSIDE: A family member isn't thinking clearly about a current problem. You can help by listening to that person's point of view rather than offering advice.

Interests

UPSIDE: You may be interested in religious or spiritual matters.

DOWNSIDE: Avoid anything to do with alcohol and drugs. You don't need them to feel good about yourself.

Health/Looks

UPSIDE: You have a good body image and a great personal style.

DOWNSIDE: You may look confident, but this is a front. You need to work on building your self-esteem.

Money

UPSIDE: You are determined to make money, and it will come to you because you are willing to work hard to get it.

DOWNSIDE: Stop daydreaming about winning the lottery. It ain't gonna happen.

30-SECOND READING

Davina recently won an award at school for best progress made. This has given her confidence a tremendous boost. She wants to know if she will pass her final exams and be accepted by a college. The card tells her that she has great energy, but if she is to make her dream come true she has to do something about it. This does not mean that it is wrong to have dreams, but rather that it is necessary to do something about them. She needs to continue to work hard and do the best that she can.

EIGHT OF CUPS

Leaning on a wand, a figure walks away from eight cups toward higher ground. We see him moving from darkness into the light. The image suggests that sometimes we need to leave situations behind, even ones that make us happy, when we know the time has come to leave. This card is all about the ability to sense when something is over and about to come crashing down around us, to know when it is time to move on.

Questions to ask yourself if you draw the Eight of Cups:

- What do you need to take time out from?
- Do you need to walk away from someone or something?
- What do you want from life?
- Might you benefit from some quiet time?
- Should you stay or should you go?

Friends

UPSIDE: You feel more in tune with some of your friends than others. Your set of close friends is about to change.

DOWNSIDE: Don't hang on to old friendships when you know deep inside that you don't have much in common anymore.

School

UPSIDE: You could be transitioning between two schools, or starting a new school year. You don't need to fear the change. In a few months' time you will feel really comfortable in your new school or class.

DOWNSIDE: You are thinking about dropping out of school. This card suggests that you should get advice from other people and take time to think, really think, about how your decision will affect the rest of your life.

Dating

UPSIDE: Are you happy in your relationship? Is the person you like really all that? Are you kidding yourself? Is it time to move on?

DOWNSIDE: Hanging on to a relationship or the idea of a relationship even when you know it isn't going to work isn't going to make you happy. Let go.

Family

UPSIDE: Family gatherings are likely.

DOWNSIDE: Don't let your fear of leaving home stop you from doing what you need to do with your life.

Interests

UPSIDE: It's time to broaden your horizons and seek out new activities that can stimulate and inspire you. Follow your heart; it will take you to the right place.

DOWNSIDE: If you don't put 100 percent into your efforts don't expect great results.

Health/Looks

UPSIDE: Your modesty and sweet nature endear you to other people.

DOWNSIDE: The time is right to go for a new look, and experiment with your personal style.

Money

UPSIDE: This is a good card for anything to do with money and work.

DOWNSIDE: If you aren't prepared to make personal sacrifices, you can't expect to have money in your pocket.

KEY THOUGHTS: Beneficial changes lie ahead, especially in personal or romantic issues. You may find yourself in a new setting, or thinking of moving. Pay attention to your intuition—that small feeling or thought or voice in your head that leaves you just knowing something, even if you don't know why.

30-SECOND READING

Lorna has an offer to go to drama school, but she loves her local high school and can't bear the thought of leaving her friends. This card suggests that it is time for her to strike out alone. She has a gift for drama and can nurture that gift at stage school. And even though she is leaving her high school, this doesn't mean she has to lose contact with her friends or discontinue her studies, because the drama school stresses the importance of academic training alongside vocational.

NINE OF CUPS

The Nine of Cups is the card of contentment and celebration. Worries and fears are avoided because the man in the picture is concentrating on the simple pleasures in life, like food, drink, and laughter. At times, especially after a period of hard work, nothing can be better than a simple good time. There is a confidence about this man. He has done his best and is congratulating himself.

Questions to ask yourself if you draw the Nine of Cups:

- Are you enjoying yourself?
- Do you count your blessings?
- Have you done your very best?
- Do you feel in control of your life?
- What dreams are being realized?

Friends

UPSIDE: Lots of party invitations and celebrations lie ahead. Enjoy yourself.

DOWNSIDE: Enjoy yourself by all means, but don't go overboard and make yourself ill.

School

UPSIDE: You may or may not be in line for a school award, but you feel very pleased with your progress over the last year. Your teachers and parents are pleased with you, too.

DOWNSIDE: You are doing well at school, but don't let it go to your head. There is far more to a person than exam grades.

Dating

UPSIDE: Hold your breath. Your dream date is about to appear.

DOWNSIDE: You may feel alone right now, whether or not you are in a relationship. Remember, until you love yourself, it is hard to feel loved by others.

Family

UPSIDE: A family celebration is likely.

DOWNSIDE: The situation at home feels oppressive. Give yourself room to breathe.

Interests

UPSIDE: Any creative project or sporting activity you have been involved in has brought you well-deserved success. Time to build on that success.

DOWNSIDE: Things are not turning out as you hoped, and you aren't getting the recognition you think you deserve. Don't give up. Try another avenue, as things will eventually go your way.

Health/Looks

UPSIDE: This is the card of good health, and with good health comes confidence and charisma.

DOWNSIDE: Unwise choices may have been made as far as health is concerned. If you want to feel and look good, review your diet, get back into regular exercise, cut down on alcohol, and stop smoking.

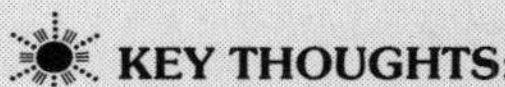

There will be success despite opposition. Don't forget to feel pleased with yourself when that success comes, and remember to take a well-earned break. Tiredness can cause physical and emotional problems. Stress can sap energy and positivity and make it hard to deal with things. Don't overdo it.

Money

UPSIDE: Any moneymaking scheme will do well.

DOWNSIDE: You may have lost some money recently or spent it unwisely. Learn from your mistake, and don't get in the same situation again.

30-SECOND READING

Brad thinks he might be gay. He feels very isolated at school and does not want to upset his family by telling them. This card is saying that he should celebrate and enjoy life. At the moment, self-loathing is having a negative effect on him and is not helping the situation. In order to accept his sexuality, he needs to concentrate on building his self-esteem so that he can like himself whether he is gay or not.

TEN OF CUPS

Ten cups form a rainbow, and below, a happy family celebrates the passing of a storm and the fine weather that follows. The rainbow suggests the feelings of relief and joy after a storm. The adults are grateful for their feelings of joy, and they look up at the rainbow. The children assume that happiness is a natural state, and play without looking up in gratitude.

Questions to ask yourself if you draw the Ten of Cups:

- Do you think you deserve happiness?
- Do you appreciate what makes you happy?
- Are you feeling grateful?
- Are you dreaming of a home and family?
- Are you sharing love and intimacy with others?

Friends

UPSIDE: You are surrounded by good friends. This is a happy time.

DOWNSIDE: Quarrels and petty jealousies are likely.

School

UPSIDE: Personal success is assured. You feel supported by your teachers and your school.

DOWNSIDE: Problems at school, but they will be short-lived.

Dating

UPSIDE: You dream of a home and family of your own. This card suggests that one day you will get all you wish for, and more.

DOWNSIDE: A feeling of sadness is likely. A permanent split may occur, or someone you like will go out with someone else. The feelings of sadness are, however, temporary.

Family

UPSIDE: A secure, loving home environment is important to you.

DOWNSIDE: There could be problems at home. You will be able to work them out.

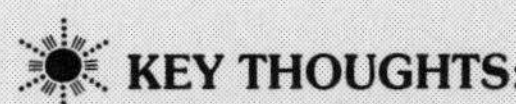

KEY THOUGHTS:

This card is love, happiness, peace, contentment, and emotional harmony. It stresses the importance of being grateful for what you already have. It also encourages you to have more fun. You'll find confidence and success come more easily and more naturally.

Interests

UPSIDE: Your interests tend to revolve around the family and home.

DOWNSIDE: Don't get so wrapped up in home and family that you forget there is a big wide world out there.

Health/Looks

UPSIDE: People are attracted to you because you radiate warmth, security, honesty, and love.

DOWNSIDE: Give yourself time to rest and relax. Try for balance. If you use your brain a lot, do something physical. If you are always busy, try doing nothing.

Money

UPSIDE: Earning your own money is important to you and gives you a feeling of security.

DOWNSIDE: Don't rely too much on other people to give you money.

30-SECOND READING

Janet feels that she needs to lose weight and wonders if she should go on a diet. This card tells her that she is fine as she is and dieting isn't necessary. She should appreciate what she has—good health—and take care of herself by being careful with what she eats and exercising regularly.

THE SUIT OF SWORDS

In many ways Swords are the most complex and difficult suit. They are associated with air, and represent the power of thought. The sword is a symbol of pain and destruction, but it can also suggest the destruction of illusion in the quest for truth. It can be the moment when things suddenly fall into place, or when you "get it." Generally Swords indicate mental activity and awareness, but they can also be signs of impending trouble—so watch out. The secret is to keep your head and think clearly. If you can do that, any problem you face will strengthen you rather than weaken you.

ACE OF SWORDS

A sword—symbol of separation, pain, analytical thinking, and discipline—is held by a hand rising from the clouds. The sword is ready to smash through any resistance. It can do this because it has no illusions. If you know what you want in life and understand the obstacles you must face, the sky really is your limit.

Questions to ask yourself if you draw the Ace of Swords:

- What change do you want to make?
- Are you getting down to essentials?
- What finally seems possible?
- Does some decision need to be made?
- What do you know you have to do?

Friends

UPSIDE: You are honest and reliable, and your friends are, too.
DOWNSIDE: You need to watch your sharp tongue. It is driving friends away from you.

School

UPSIDE: You are, or soon will be, top of the class if you keep working hard.
DOWNSIDE: If you spend your time looking out of the classroom window rather than at the teacher, don't be surprised when your results are poor.

Dating

UPSIDE: Someone inspires in you a passion and determination you have not encountered before.
DOWNSIDE: Misunderstandings cause confusion. It's time to find out where you stand.

Family

UPSIDE: Things are changing for the better.

DOWNSIDE: A time of mental stress and anxiety. Watch your temper.

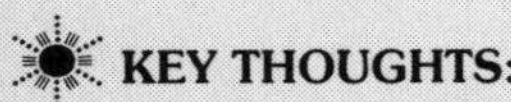

KEY THOUGHTS:

Act with integrity, discipline, and firmness in order to succeed. Use all your powers of concentration. If you are frightened of something or someone, imagine that person or thing in a funny or harmless context, reduced in size, or as a cartoon sketch. Give your fear a name and a face. Talk to it. Tell it to get out of your life. Watch it fade away.

Interests

UPSIDE: You are about to take charge of a group, and it will thrive under your leadership.

DOWNSIDE: You are getting involved with activities you don't understand or feel comfortable with. It would be wise to rethink what you're doing.

Health/Looks

UPSIDE: You have had health or weight problems recently but are tackling them successfully.

DOWNSIDE: Apathy is your downfall. If you don't make an effort with your appearance, why should you expect other people to make an effort for you?

Money

UPSIDE: Nothing can stand in your way at the moment. You will find ways to earn extra cash.

DOWNSIDE: Clashes with authority figures could limit your earning potential.

30-SECOND READING

Sonia has had health problems for as long as she can remember. Her diabetes and bouts of asthma make it hard for her to keep up at school. The Ace of Swords tells her that she has the determination and willpower to manage her problems. Her courage and strength in the face of adversity will take her far in life.

TWO OF SWORDS

A woman with a blindfold sits with her back to the water and holds two swords across her chest. At any moment she could lose her balance and fall forward or backward, but she remains tense and rigid between both possibilities. This is a card of avoidance, not confusion. The figure has obviously tied her blindfold on herself so she doesn't have to decide which way to go. Why?

Questions to ask yourself if you draw the Two of Swords:

- What decision needs to be made?
- What or who are you avoiding?
- Why are you buying time?
- Why are you hesitating?
- What don't you want to admit to yourself?

Friends

UPSIDE: Time to make a decision about whom you want to spend your time with.

DOWNSIDE: Some of your friends aren't being honest to you, or perhaps you are lying to yourself.

School

UPSIDE: Clear choices need to be made about which subjects you want to concentrate on.

DOWNSIDE: You aren't making as much progress as you could. Find out why you are unwilling to put in the effort. If you don't understand, ask for help. If you are frightened of failing, the only way to overcome that fear is to face it. If you are being bullied in any way, talk to your parents immediately.

Dating

UPSIDE: You know that dating two people at once is not a good idea. Time to decide whom you want.

DOWNSIDE: If you let no one approach you, you won't be hurt, but such a defensive approach to life isn't going to bring happiness.

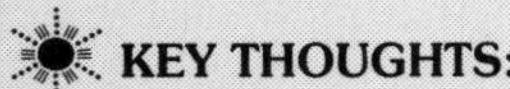

KEY THOUGHTS: End the stalemate so things can move forward with your life and you can feel more able to deal with the situation. Use your creativity to help you reach your goals.

Family

UPSIDE: Family rifts will be resolved, and you will be surrounded by affection.

DOWNSIDE: Clashes with your parents or guardians are in the cards. You are lashing out at anyone who is close to you, but underneath your anger there is hurt and confusion. Don't be afraid to open up to those who care about you.

Interests

UPSIDE: You could be getting interested in meditation or other ways to quiet your mind.

DOWNSIDE: There is too little going on in your life outside school and home. Find something that motivates and inspires you. Do you enjoy math or science? Would you like to learn about other countries? Are you interested in crime or detective novels? The possibilities are endless for someone as creative as you.

Health/Looks

UPSIDE: You are blessed with good looks. Others may envy you.

DOWNSIDE: Don't hide all the time. Let the world see who you are.

Money

UPSIDE: You are putting aside money for a rainy day.

DOWNSIDE: Money isn't the answer to all your problems. It can't take away the pain you feel.

30-SECOND READING

Tania has ballet and piano class scheduled on the same night. What can she do? This card indicates that she needs to make a clear choice. She should do what she enjoys most rather than what she feels will impress others. Whatever she decides to commit herself to she will do well in. The important thing is to make a decision about where she is going, in order to focus her energies.

THREE OF SWORDS

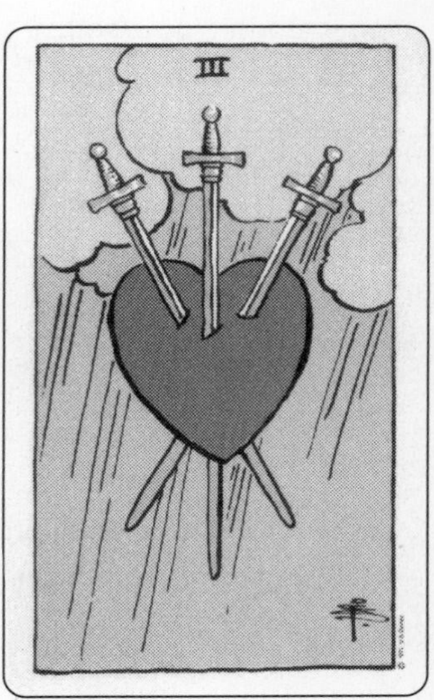

The Three of Swords is the card of sorrow and heartache. When upsetting or disappointing things happen in life—when a loved one dies, when you fail a crucial exam—it is important that you allow yourself to feel the pain. You shouldn't pretend everything is fine and ignore the pain inside. If you do this you carry the pain forever in your heart. Far better to release the pain and then move forward.

Questions to ask yourself if you draw the Three of Swords:

- Are you in pain?
- Have you lost something or someone important to you?
- Do you feel betrayed?
- Are you releasing your pain?
- Are you hurting someone? Are you hurting yourself?

Friends

UPSIDE: You have left your friends behind, or will do so soon, as you pursue your goals. You will miss them, but you are very excited about what the future will bring.

DOWNSIDE: You feel incompatible with your friends. Remind yourself that we all feel different and isolated at times. It's part of growing up.

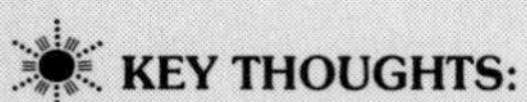

KEY THOUGHTS: What you are encountering is necessary for you to progress, but it won't be easy. If you feel frightened, take slow breaths and focus on calming yourself. This will help you process information through the logical, rational part of your brain, and you'll deal with the situation more easily and with better results.

School

UPSIDE: Grades and reports have not been great recently, but you are determined to make amends and improve your work.

DOWNSIDE: You may be starting at a new school or joining a new class. It won't be easy settling in at first, but give it time. The situation will improve.

Dating

UPSIDE: There could be disappointment in love, but it is only temporary. Things will improve.

DOWNSIDE: You are eaten up with sorrow about a relationship that hasn't worked out.

Family

UPSIDE: A recent upset at home has brought the family closer together.

DOWNSIDE: A family member may have passed away or moved to a new area.

Interests

UPSIDE: An all-consuming interest, possibly in computers or some kind of engineering work or research, is taking up a lot of time. This could lead to exciting new developments.

DOWNSIDE: Numbing your pain with mindless distractions won't help. It is important to face your pain right now, not avoid it.

Health/Looks

UPSIDE: You aren't pressuring yourself to be perfect anymore, and this new, relaxed attitude yields positive results.

DOWNSIDE: If you are harming yourself in any way, please seek medical advice.

Money

UPSIDE: This is a great time to sort out your finances.

DOWNSIDE: There will be delays and disappointments.

30-SECOND READING

Colleen has just broken up with a guy. Will she get back with him? This card is indicating the heartache and upset she is going through. It tells her that there will be no reconciliation. She has to come to terms with her loss and put it behind her. This won't be easy, but she has the inner strength to do it.

FOUR OF SWORDS

In the Four of Swords we see the image of a body resting, in contrast to the vivid scene outside the window. Someone has decided to take time out or retreat from the world. Sometimes we respond to difficulties by withdrawing or literally hiding in our rooms. Withdrawal can lead to healing, if the purpose is not to hide but to recoup strength. Problems occur only if withdrawal starts to shut out the world.

Questions to ask yourself if you draw the Four of Swords:

- What are you hiding from?
- Are you taking some time out?
- Are you waiting for someone to rescue you?

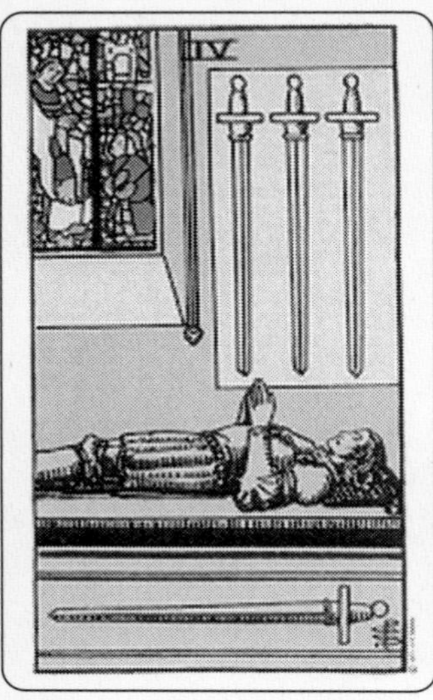

- Are you thinking things through?
- Do you feel cut off?

Friends

UPSIDE: Your friends have, or will be, a great support to you in times of trouble.

DOWNSIDE: You feel isolated. Have your friends deserted you?

School

UPSIDE: You want more time alone to concentrate on your schoolwork.

DOWNSIDE: You are being forced out of various school activities. Try to find out why.

KEY THOUGHTS: If you need to retreat from the troubles of life, make sure you retreat to recuperate, not withdraw. Too much withdrawal can shut you off from the world, creating a spell that only other people can break. Make sure you find balance in your life between resting and working, thinking and acting, being and doing.

Dating

UPSIDE: Now is a good time to enjoy a period of rest or recovery from emotional problems.

DOWNSIDE: Give yourself time to mourn the loss of a relationship. Don't expect someone else to take away the hurt that you feel. It isn't fair to them.

Family

UPSIDE: A vacation or period of rest is advisable for your family so everyone can recharge their batteries.

DOWNSIDE: You find family life restrictive, but things will improve.

Interests

UPSIDE: Your love of reading and reflection is a source of great strength.

DOWNSIDE: Too much noise is draining your energy, not to mention the damage it is doing to your eardrums.

Health/Looks

UPSIDE: You are a trendsetter. People follow your lead in the fashion stakes.

DOWNSIDE: There could be visits to hospitals, but not necessarily a personal illness.

Money

UPSIDE: Money is scarce right now, but in time the situation will improve.

DOWNSIDE: You may find it hard to get a job. It might be better to concentrate on your studies for a while, and then look again.

30-SECOND READING

Derek and his family have moved five times in the past three years. Finally his parents have decided to settle in an area, and he won't have to change schools again. This card suggests a welcome period of rest for Derek in which he can concentrate on his schoolwork and build friendships without having to worry that he will have to say goodbye and start all over again somewhere else.

FIVE OF SWORDS

The Five of Swords is another card of pain and loss. But what do you identify with in the card—the man in the front who has won the battle, or the two disappointed men walking away? The card also isn't as straightforward as it seems. One of the great things about growing up is that you begin to see that nothing in life is black and white, and all things will change. Perhaps the two men walking away refused to fight for something they didn't believe in. They may not look like winners, but they really are. Or perhaps they did lose the battle this time, but revenge motivates them to fight and win the next time.

Questions to ask yourself if you draw the Five of Swords:

- How important is winning for you?
- Do you believe in what you are fighting for?
- Whom are you bullying, or who is bullying you?
- Do you feel like a winner or a loser?
- Who is threatening you, or whom are you threatening?

Friends

UPSIDE: Partings may occur, a friend may leave the country, but new friendships are also indicated.

DOWNSIDE: Watch for troublemakers, violence, and arguments.

School

UPSIDE: You realize that you have problems at school but have decided to stand and face up to them.

DOWNSIDE: Bullying is an issue. If you are the bully, stop it. If you are being bullied, talk to your teachers now.

Dating

UPSIDE: You have got the guy or girl of your dreams, but is this person really all that you thought they were?

DOWNSIDE: A relationship may have come to an end. Mingled with sadness, you also feel relief.

Family

UPSIDE: An end to family feuds. Cut your losses and swallow your pride.

DOWNSIDE: You are working against your family in every possible way. Is it making you happy?

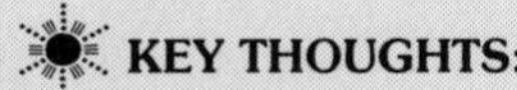

KEY THOUGHTS:

Face up to your problems and deal with them. It won't be easy, but you will win in the end. Develop your assertiveness. Assertive people aren't aggressive people; they remain calm and in control, and they refuse to let other people intimidate them. Slow, deep, and regular breathing is vital. Remember, it is important to stay in control.

Interests

UPSIDE: You love to win, and thrive at competitive sports or activities.

DOWNSIDE: You show a certain stubborn pride and a refusal to give in, even when all is lost.

Health/Looks

UPSIDE: You feel great about yourself right now. You look great, too.

DOWNSIDE: Don't let the hurtful comments of others drag you down.

Money

UPSIDE: A change in direction is necessary if you want to improve your earning power.

DOWNSIDE: Guard against taking on too much work and not being able to cope. Watch for possible theft.

30-SECOND READING

Trisha feels that her teacher picks on her. The Five of Swords says that Trisha should not confront her teacher because she can't win this battle. Her best approach would be to stop giving her teacher ammunition and find out what she can do to limit the criticism. If late assignments are an issue, she should make sure she hands them in on time. If wearing jewelry in class is an issue, she should leave her jewelry at home, and so on. Once Trisha changes

(continued)

her behavior, the chances are she will get praise instead of criticism. If she still feels she is picked on, then would be the time to take matters to her counselor, the department head, or the principal.

SIX OF SWORDS

On this card we see a ferryman carrying passengers to the other shore. Notice that all the swords are balanced in the boat, suggesting that stability has returned after a period of difficulty. The ferryman, who represents our spirit, is guiding the figures—our personality and body—to another stage in our life.

Questions to ask yourself if you draw the Six of Swords:

- Are you moving on to something new?
- Is this a good time to back off?
- What or who are you escaping?
- Are you changing direction?
- Do you feel like you are being carried to safety?

Friends

UPSIDE: A quiet, restful time for you and your friends lies ahead.
DOWNSIDE: Lack of communication between you and your friends will cause problems.

School

UPSIDE: You are about to start a new course of study.
DOWNSIDE: You are giving up too easily.

Dating

UPSIDE: You are about to start a new relationship or to significantly improve the one you are in.
DOWNSIDE: Until you learn from your mistakes, relationships will be unsatisfying.

Family

UPSIDE: A family move is indicated. It will work out very well.
DOWNSIDE: You have to let go of past grudges. They are dragging you and your family down.

Interests

UPSIDE: There may be trips abroad, or a visitor from another country.
DOWNSIDE: Too much silence in your life. Get out more.

Health/Looks

UPSIDE: You are taking good care of yourself and making sure that you lead a balanced, healthy life.
DOWNSIDE: You will experience poor health as the result of stress.

Money

UPSIDE: Money is scarce, but you are coping well with the situation.
DOWNSIDE: Watch your finances. This is not a good card for money-making activities.

KEY THOUGHTS:
You are moving from stormy seas to tranquility. Make sure you go in a positive direction and stay confident, calm, and secure in your identity. Stay in control and remind yourself that you are in charge of your thoughts and feelings. You decide how you react to a situation. You can lose your cool, get angry, or curl up and cry, or you can assert yourself effectively in your everyday life.

30-SECOND READING
Conrad has been asked to leave the school tennis team. The card is saying that there is no point in crying over spilled milk; what is done is done. He does, however, need to find out what

(continued)

the problem is so he can learn from his mistakes and move forward. It is not necessarily the end of his tennis career. He may just need a new approach.

SEVEN OF SWORDS

A man is in the process of carrying five swords, but he looks back at the two he has left behind. Because he looks back while moving forward, the image suggests that he is leaving something behind and he isn't sure he has made the right decision. The theme of struggle continues with this card. Action has been taken, but better planning may have been needed beforehand.

Questions to ask yourself if you draw the Seven of Swords:

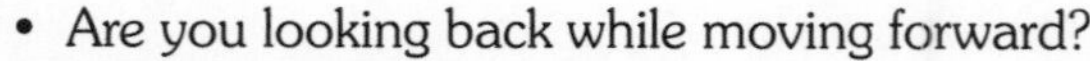

- Are you looking back while moving forward?
- What is holding you back?
- What are you leaving behind?
- Are you taking a risk?
- What do you think you are getting away with?

Friends

UPSIDE: You are leaving some friends behind as you move forward with your life.

DOWNSIDE: Don't give your trust too readily.

School

UPSIDE: Sometimes you just need to be self-reliant and get on with things. This is one of those times.

DOWNSIDE: Cheating is never a good thing.

Dating

UPSIDE: A new relationship awaits you. Have confidence that it will work out.

DOWNSIDE: An old relationship or crush is holding you back. Set your heart free.

Family

UPSIDE: Your parents or guardians work hard and sacrifice much to give you the best that they can. Make sure you show your appreciation.

DOWNSIDE: Stop living in the past, and focus on the future instead.

Interests

UPSIDE: This is a card of ambition and effort. New hopes, plans, and aims are coming. You may be drawn toward writing, law, or the secret service.

DOWNSIDE: You will face disappointment, and advice given may not be sound.

Health/Looks

UPSIDE: If you want to look your very best, sometimes you have to try new things.

DOWNSIDE: Are you taking good care of yourself? What aspect of your health are you neglecting: diet, exercise, sleep?

Money

UPSIDE: A calculated risk will pay off.

DOWNSIDE: Are you taking something or spending money that isn't yours?

KEY THOUGHTS:
Things are going on that are not what they seem. Something may have to be sacrificed in order for you to succeed or move forward with your life. This can mean giving up the herd mentality and being true to yourself. You may have gone along with your friends, even when you knew it was wrong, because you didn't want to be different. Standing up against your friends or the crowd demands confidence, self-assurance, and assertiveness. You really have to be strong.

30-SECOND READING

Dolly is helping to care for a sick relative. At the same time she has her exams to focus on, as well as a part-time job. She feels exhausted most of the time. The card is saying that she is doing too much. She will have to do less than she is doing now. She will feel regret, but if she doesn't find some kind of compromise, she will burn herself out.

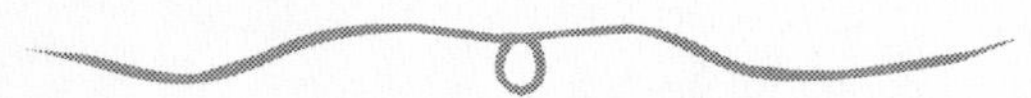

EIGHT OF SWORDS

The Eight of Swords isn't as bad as it looks. Yes, a woman is blindfolded and surrounded by swords, but notice that the swords do not fence her in, the ropes hang loosely around her legs, and the people who have blindfolded her do not appear in the card. There is nothing to prevent her from just leaving. The clue to this card is the blindfold. Once she can take that off, she will be able to see her situation clearly. Questions to ask yourself if you draw the Eight of Swords:

- What's stopping you?
- What are you blinding yourself to?
- What are you almost free of?
- Is your mind closed or open?
- How can you get out of your self-imposed prison?

Friends

UPSIDE: Friends are helping you through a difficult time.
DOWNSIDE: You feel alone and friendless and can't see a way out.

School

UPSIDE: You may not want to cause trouble by asking for the help you need, but you must ask anyway.
DOWNSIDE: You are being subjected to unjust criticism. Remain strong.

Dating

UPSIDE: You are starting to stand up for yourself in relationships. Good for you.
DOWNSIDE: Are you trapped in a difficult relationship?

Family

UPSIDE: Things aren't ideal at home, but you are making progress.
DOWNSIDE: You feel trapped and oppressed at home. Be patient. The time will soon come when you can spread your wings.

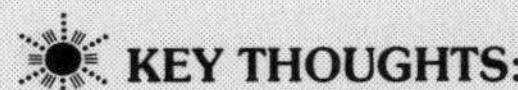

KEY THOUGHTS:

Restrictions will lift and setbacks will be temporary if you take the initiative and work toward finding a solution. It may also help to stop being so serious. Humor and imagination help us learn and understand.

Interests

UPSIDE: You have found an interest that you really enjoy.
DOWNSIDE: You have had problems fitting in when you tried to join in with various social activities. You will eventually find the right group for you.

Health/Looks

UPSIDE: You are feeling much better after a period of poor health or stress.
DOWNSIDE: You may be suffering stress-related problems. Take it easy for a while.

Money

UPSIDE: Financial restrictions will be temporary. The situation will soon improve.

DOWNSIDE: Watch out for accidents or financial loss.

30-SECOND READING

Esperanza is being bullied by her friends because they think she is fat. What can she do? This card is saying that a solution can be found. She needs to work on her self-confidence as well as weight management. This means taking the initiative and working on building her self-esteem while at the same time sticking to a healthful eating and exercise program.

NINE OF SWORDS

A woman sits crying in bed with her head in her hands. Or is she praying? Nine swords hang over her head. The image suggests how painful it can be sometimes to accept that you can't always have what you want. The swords aren't hurting her—they hang in the air—so this could indicate that someone she cares about is in pain or that the pain is only imagined, not real. This card makes us ask if we can see a way out of such dreadful pain.

Questions to ask yourself if you draw the Nine of Swords:

- Why do you feel so sad?
- What are you coming to terms with?
- Are you agonizing over a decision?
- Do you take on the sorrows of the world?
- Do you feel misunderstood?

Friends

UPSIDE: Disagreements with a friend will clear the air, and in the long run will produce a happier friendship.

DOWNSIDE: Lots of arguing and name-calling are upsetting everybody and making the situation worse. Time to find a compromise or walk away.

School

UPSIDE: You are worrying a great deal about exam results. Don't. It will be fine in the end.

DOWNSIDE: Your constant worrying is creating problems not just for you, but for your parents.

Dating

UPSIDE: Lack of self-confidence is the only thing holding you back.

DOWNSIDE: You may be experiencing anxiety and sleepless nights. He or she isn't worth it.

Family

UPSIDE: Try to be positive for your family at this difficult time.

DOWNSIDE: Family problems may feel overwhelming. Make sure you find someone you trust whom you can confide in.

Interests

UPSIDE: Find something that can take your mind off things for a while. Read a good book, go for a walk, write a short story, draw a picture, bake a cake—there's no end to the activities that can keep you occupied.

KEY THOUGHTS:

You may feel like you are doing something when you worry, but the truth is, worry achieves nothing. All it does is make you ill. If there is something you can do about the situation, do it. If there is nothing you can do, let the worry go. Most of the time what we worry about doesn't happen anyway. Stop wasting time worrying, and start living instead.

DOWNSIDE: Being fearful leads to its own problems, and you need to look into yourself to see where the problem is.

Health/Looks

UPSIDE: If you feel positive about yourself, you will look and feel great.
DOWNSIDE: A card of illness and poor health due to stress and anxiety.

Money

UPSIDE: Recovery from financial loss will be swift.
DOWNSIDE: A card of financial loss.

30-SECOND READING

Janice is worried about her friend Darlene, who has panic attacks on a regular basis. Things have gotten so bad that Darlene often misses school. The card indicates that Darlene is in no fit state to help herself. It is up to her parents now to get her on a course of treatment. Janice can offer practical and emotional support to Darlene, but she must do this without getting too involved. Things are out of her hands, and Janice needs to put the focus back on her own life.

TEN OF SWORDS

Ten swords have pierced a man. Think about it—isn't it a bit much? It only takes one sword to kill someone. We often tend to exaggerate our problems and make more of them than they really are. We use dramatic statements like "It's a disaster" when it isn't, or "this is the end," when clearly it isn't. Look closely at this card: There is light on the horizon. The situation isn't as bad as you think it is.

Questions to ask yourself if you draw the Ten of Swords:

- What has struck you down?
- Do you feel overwhelmed?
- What are you being forced to accept?
- Do you feel helpless?
- What's crushing your ego?

Friends

UPSIDE: Your friends go from one crisis to another. You are always the one who pulls everyone through.

DOWNSIDE: Friendships are breaking down. There may be tears, grief, and unhappiness. This is only temporary. Things will improve.

School

UPSIDE: Things aren't as bad as they seem. Your situation will soon improve if you work hard enough.

DOWNSIDE: You go into meltdown over little things, like losing your pencil case or forgetting to wear your watch. Get a sense of perspective if you want to be taken seriously.

Dating

UPSIDE: Some kind of parting or separation is in the cards, but it is necessary for a better relationship to be formed.

DOWNSIDE: Your advances may recently have been rejected, and you are nursing a bruised ego. Don't worry; you will get your confidence back soon.

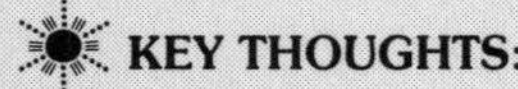

KEY THOUGHTS:

Unwelcome changes will occur and they will be difficult to cope with, but you *will* cope and come through the experience feeling more positive and more capable. No experience is ever wasted if you learn from it. Be optimistic. Find something hopeful to focus on. If you fail your exams, you can always try again. If your parents split up, at least there will be no more arguments and tension. By sheer willpower, you can find something positive in any situation.

Family

UPSIDE: Things aren't as bad as you think they are.

DOWNSIDE: Stay positive in the face of difficulties. Seek support from friends or teachers if you need to.

Interests

UPSIDE: Look for things that uplift you. You may have lost a battle but you can still win the war.

DOWNSIDE: What are you learning about yourself from the problems and setbacks you are facing?

Health/Looks

UPSIDE: You are starting to like yourself a little more. Now the only way to go is up.

DOWNSIDE: Don't let negative thinking set in. You are terrific.

Money

UPSIDE: A slight improvement in your finances.

DOWNSIDE: Be watchful of people who may try to encourage you to spend money you haven't got.

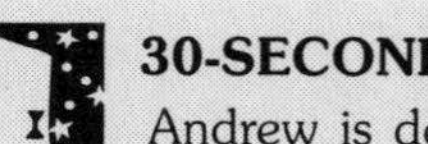

30-SECOND READING

Andrew is devastated. His parents have divorced and he finds it hard to come to terms with the new arrangement—weekdays with mom, weekends with dad. This card indicates that Andrew is hurting badly, but in time he will see that the situation is better for all concerned. Right now he needs a lot of support from friends and family, and should not try to go through this alone.

THE SUIT OF PENTACLES

The Pentacles represent the element of earth and practical, down-to-earth matters. They are generally associated with material things, like work, money, and business. The Pentacles carry the problem of becoming so involved with the material and practical side of things that we forget about the emotional and spiritual, but if we can unite a love for material things with a love for the world around us, the Pentacles can bring the joy of satisfying work into our lives.

ACE OF PENTACLES

A pentacle—symbol of the material world—is cradled in a hand coming out of the clouds. One of the big lessons of growing up is learning to handle money well, be it money from your parents or money you earn from a part-time job. This card tells us that money is a gift that can bring security, order, and great joy into our lives, but only if we don't let it corrupt us. We must learn to respect money and use it wisely.

Questions to ask yourself if you draw the Ace of Pentacles:

- Do you handle money well?
- What does having enough money mean to you?

- Have you come into some money recently?
- Do you respect money?
- Are you prospering?

Friends

UPSIDE: A friend will soon put you in touch with someone who will offer you an opportunity to make extra money.

DOWNSIDE: One or more of your friends is costing you too much. Think carefully about spending your time, and your money, with them.

School

UPSIDE: It has suddenly become important to you to relate your schoolwork to the real world outside. Talk to your parents and teachers, and they will be more than willing to offer you advice.

DOWNSIDE: Is there some time-wasting going on at school?

KEY THOUGHTS:

Financial success is in the cards, but don't become selfish, competitive, and overdependent on security and comfort. In other words, enjoy wealth without letting it go to your head.

Dating

UPSIDE: You have a partner, or need to look for one, who shares your love of the good things in life.

DOWNSIDE: You can't buy someone's love.

Family

UPSIDE: Someone in your family will get an exciting job offer.

DOWNSIDE: Someone in your family has become greedy and mean. Don't let it get to you.

Interests

UPSIDE: You will be blessed with an abundance of energy and the drive and determination to work for your goals.

DOWNSIDE: Stop wasting money on things you don't really need.

Health/Looks

UPSIDE: Someone is having a profound effect on your personal style. You will benefit from their advice.

DOWNSIDE: Copy, by all means, but don't lose a sense of your own identity.

Money

UPSIDE: You will be offered a job or moneymaking opportunity in the near future. There is also the possibility of a legacy.

DOWNSIDE: Gambles may be profitable, but your success will not make you happy.

30-SECOND READING

Sean worries about his parents. They are always working. This card indicates that family life is out of balance and it would be a good idea if Sean took the initiative and talked to his parents. Once they realize that seeing more of them is more important to him than new running shoes or flashy presents at Christmas, they will work toward some kind of compromise.

TWO OF PENTACLES

A juggler is trying to juggle two pentacles, and behind him a ship is being tossed and turned by the waves. This tells us that much of life is beyond our control, but also that we can control the way we react.

We need to stay balanced in the midst of life's ups and downs. Like many Pentacles, this card suggests hidden magic in ordinary pleasures. The juggler is enjoying his game. We learn not only in serious moments; fun and laughter can also teach us a great deal, as long as we pay attention.

Questions to ask yourself if you draw the Two of Pentacles:

- Do you feel as if you are juggling your life?
- Are you being pulled in too many directions?
- Is it hard for you to keep a sense of balance?
- What options are you considering?
- Do you feel anxious about the uncertainties of life, or are you in control?

Friends

UPSIDE: Friends are putting you under pressure, and you are balancing conflicting demands well.
DOWNSIDE: Don't put on a front and pretend everything is okay when it isn't.

School

UPSIDE: Well done. You are juggling your responsibilities well.
DOWNSIDE: School is too low of a priority at the moment. Get some balance back in your life by focusing more on schoolwork, and less on your friends.

Dating

UPSIDE: Everything is up in the air at the moment in your relationship. It could go either way. Much depends on what you decide you want to do.
DOWNSIDE: Too much indecision and uncertainty is destroying your chance of happiness.

Family

UPSIDE: You are balancing conflicting demands within and outside of your family amazingly well.

DOWNSIDE: You are doing too much and neglecting certain members of your family. You can never get back the time you should have spent with someone you love.

Interests

UPSIDE: So many interests, so little time. You are someone who is never bored.

DOWNSIDE: Don't spread yourself too thin.

Health/Looks

UPSIDE: You understand the importance of balancing the pleasure of eating what you want with the importance of physical health—eating what is good for you.

DOWNSIDE: Don't push yourself too hard on the exercise front. Everything in moderation. Be kind to your body: eat healthful food, drink lots of water, and get the right amount of exercise and sleep. Being healthy and feeling good will help you think more clearly and improve your performance.

KEY THOUGHTS:

Moderation is key in life. If it is success you are after, if you want to make the most of your opportunities, then you must be aware of the needs of your body, mind, and soul. It's a matter of finding the balance between fun and looking after yourself—the balance that's right for you and helps you to get the most out of your life.

Money

UPSIDE: Circumstances will improve slowly, and you will have to be very clever in using your funds to your best advantage.

DOWNSIDE: New moneymaking ideas will be slow starters, and you will feel anxious about the out come. You may also be in a situation in which money has to be paid to a partner or a friend.

30-SECOND READING

Angela has two friends who hate each other. Whom should she spend the most time with? This card is saying that she should not have to make a choice. Her friends need to recognize that they are being immature and should stop trying to control her. If they can't do this, she is better off without them.

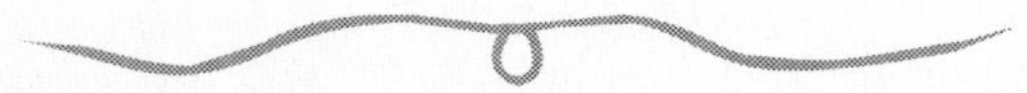

THREE OF PENTACLES

A sculptor is working in a church or monastery. His work is being admired, suggesting that he is getting the recognition he deserves. The monks who admire his work are also keen to learn. It is important to have good role models in life. The Three of Pentacles suggests success through hard work and effort.

Questions to ask yourself if you draw the Three of Pentacles:

- Do you love your work?
- Are you working hard?
- Are you training for something?
- Are you getting recognition for your work?
- Are you setting standards for yourself?

Friends

UPSIDE: One of your friends, possibly someone a little older than you, has a very positive influence on you.

DOWNSIDE: You are surrounding yourself with poor role models. Seek out friends who inspire and challenge you, not those who drag you down.

School

UPSIDE: You'll have an opportunity to show off your skills. Take it, and enjoy the praise you will get.

DOWNSIDE: You are lacking in ideas and motivation. Indifference and laziness should be guarded against.

Dating

UPSIDE: It's great that you are not following peer pressure. Keep your high standards as far as relationships are concerned. You deserve the best and should wait until you find it.

DOWNSIDE: You have a tendency to be critical, and this can intimidate potential partners. Back off a little, and show your softer side.

KEY THOUGHTS:

This card suggests success through hard work and effort. Don't wait for the mood to do things to hit you. Just keep working away at it, and success will come.

Family

UPSIDE: You come from a dedicated, hard-working family and are a credit to them.

DOWNSIDE: Lack of cooperation among family members could cause tension.

Interests

UPSIDE: This is the card of the artist, tradesperson, or builder, and it augurs well for any do-it-yourself scheme at home. Hard work will be necessary, but the result looks more than promising.

DOWNSIDE: You are great at starting things, but not so good at finishing them. Try sticking to things a bit more.

Health/Looks

UPSIDE: You take a lot of care with your appearance and should be proud of the results.

DOWNSIDE: What goes on in your mind has an effect on your body, and what goes on in your body has an effect on your mind. Take care of yourself.

Money

UPSIDE: You should have success in moneymaking matters.

DOWNSIDE: You are likely to find yourself short of funds.

30-SECOND READING

Lance isn't doing well at school. When is his work going to turn around? The card is saying that this is really up to him. No magic fairy is going to turn up and do his work for him. He needs to make more effort and apply himself more. Success won't happen overnight, but it will come in the long run if he is committed to it.

FOUR OF PENTACLES

The image on the Four of Pentacles suggests a preoccupation with material things and a desire to hold on to what you have. You will notice that the man has pentacles all around him, but has not been able to cover his back. This tells us that no matter how hard you try to protect yourself, the unexpected can still strike. The man's position—outside the city—suggests that he must take care of himself before he can take care of others, but there is also the possibility that he is strengthening himself to help others less fortunate.

Questions to ask yourself if you draw the Four of Pentacles:

- What are you afraid of losing?
- Is someone trying to take something or someone from you?

- What does having enough mean to you?
- What would make you feel secure in a changing world?
- What are you protecting or defending?

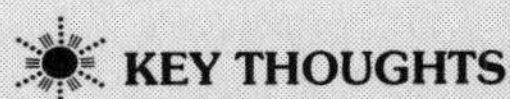

Be sure to be reasonably generous with those around you, and with yourself. You may fear loss, but you have nothing to fear except fear itself. Make yourself feel special. If you value and appreciate yourself, others will see the difference and respond to it. It will help improve your confidence and your ability.

Friends

UPSIDE: You are helping your friends with their problems. Don't forget your own.

DOWNSIDE: You aren't very generous with your friends, and this has been noticed.

School

UPSIDE: You are focused on your studies, which is good, but don't forget to give yourself time to relax.

DOWNSIDE: Cheating on exams is not the way to get ahead. Don't even think about it.

Dating

UPSIDE: When you're in a relationship, don't suffocate your partner with jealousy.

DOWNSIDE: Stop being so controlling. It will drive people away, not bring them closer.

Family

UPSIDE: You and your family don't need to feel insecure. Everything will be fine.

DOWNSIDE: There is very little sharing and compromising at home.

Interests

UPSIDE: Lack of money shouldn't keep you from having fun. The best things in life are free.

DOWNSIDE: Don't get too preoccupied with material things.

Health/Looks

UPSIDE: You look like a million dollars.

DOWNSIDE: If you don't feel good inside you won't look good, no matter how much money you spend on clothes and haircuts.

Money

UPSIDE: This is the card of King Midas, the love of wealth and luxury. You will get some extra money, but will put it away for a rainy day. Remember that money isn't everything; while we need financial and material security, there are others matters of equal or greater importance in life.

DOWNSIDE: Watch your spending, as there is a tendency to spend money you do not have.

30-SECOND READING

Majel is going to a party tomorrow, and is fretting about what to wear. She pulls a Tarot card, and gets the Four of Pentacles as a warning. The cards like to be treated with a certain amount of respect. It's far better to take an important decision to the cards than a superficial one. If Majel continues her superficial approach to life, she will get herself into trouble.

FIVE OF PENTACLES

Two beggars trudge through the snow and cold. Physical hardship and misery dominate the picture. Yet shelter and help are at hand, as the beggars are near a church. All they need to do is find the door.

Questions to ask yourself if you draw the Five of Pentacles:

- Do you feel like an outcast?
- What comforts are you doing without?
- Whom might you ask for help?
- What is crippling you?
- Are you too proud to accept assistance?

Friends

UPSIDE: Welcome new students to your school with enthusiasm and confidence.

DOWNSIDE: You may treat newcomers with indifference or shyly keep out of their way. Neither of these approaches is good.

School

UPSIDE: Work isn't easy for you at the moment. Don't forget, help is at hand from your teachers, but you have to ask for it. Don't fear things because they are difficult. See them as opportunities to learn new and useful things.

DOWNSIDE: Step back from the brink before it is too late, and start paying attention in class.

Dating

UPSIDE: A friend may be doing some matchmaking without you realizing it.

DOWNSIDE: There could be difficulties with close relationships right now, but things will eventually turn out well.

Family

UPSIDE: Your family is scrimping and saving at the moment, but it will be worth it in the end.

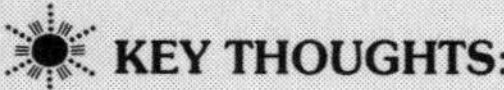

KEY THOUGHTS:

A solution to your problems could be found, if only you would look around for it. Don't get accustomed to suffering, and don't shut out help when it is offered. Rise to the challenge and draw on your inner strength. Act, don't react. Direct the circumstances of your life rather than respond to them. Be proactive. This means you take action to change your life rather than having to respond to events when they occur. When you take control, you increase your confidence and overcome your fears.

DOWNSIDE: Constant arguments about money poison the atmosphere.

Interests

UPSIDE: You have a positive attitude about new things, and learn new skills fast.

DOWNSIDE: You tend to get stuck in a rut. Why not welcome change as a new adventure, a new opportunity to develop your potential? Take the action you need to take. When opportunity presents itself, don't run away from it.

Health/Looks

UPSIDE: You may be feeling insecure about yourself, but friends and family will offer emotional support.

DOWNSIDE: Be realistic. You cannot live in the past. Styles and sizes that you wore a few years ago won't suit or fit you now.

Money

UPSIDE: Things are finally turning around for you financially.

DOWNSIDE: This is not a good card for money matters. Watch your spending.

30-SECOND READING

Jeanie is wondering if she should open an account at the store that sells her favorite clothes and shoes. This card gives her a strong warning. Jeannie should wait until she has the security of a job behind her before she makes financial commitments.

SIX OF PENTACLES

The Six of Pentacles is a card of sharing. A well-dressed man weighs money in a pair of scales, giving it to those in need. The scale suggests that the help you get in life comes at the precise time that you need it. Think about this book. You picked it up because you are starting to ask the big questions in life. If you had come across this book five or ten years ago, you would not have been able to understand it. You would not have been ready then. You are reading it now because you are ready to understand it.

Questions to ask yourself if you draw the Six of Pentacles:

- What are you giving?
- What are you receiving?
- Are you giving too much?
- Are you receiving too much?
- What are you sharing or in need of?

Friends

UPSIDE: A friend of yours is in trouble. Luckily, you are there to help.
DOWNSIDE: Whom are you bribing, or who is bribing you?

School

UPSIDE: There is one teacher in particular who brings out the best in you.
DOWNSIDE: Stop comparing yourself with others in your class. The only person you should be competing against is yourself.

Dating

UPSIDE: You are one of life's givers, and it isn't hard for you to get dates. Try saying no a little more often.

DOWNSIDE: Why are you being so hurtful and hurting someone who really cares about you?

Family

UPSIDE: The generosity and love you experience at home have rubbed off on you, and you are likely to offer support when it is needed by those you care about.

DOWNSIDE: You are just taking and taking without giving anything back. Stop being so selfish.

KEY THOUGHTS:

Giving is a win-win situation. Through giving to others, you will receive. The other person gets the help they need, and you feel good about helping them. This improves your confidence and self-esteem, which in turn helps you create your own success.

Interests

UPSIDE: You are getting more involved in projects, and meeting adults who are powerful role models. This is the card of charity work, altruism, and kindness.

DOWNSIDE: You don't realize how talented you are. Don't hide your light under a barrel. Let the world see how much you have to offer it.

Health/Looks

UPSIDE: Your sense of style is the envy of all your friends.

DOWNSIDE: Guard against the envy of others. You will be the loser if these emotions take hold.

Money

UPSIDE: It feels great to have paid your debts, and you are determined not to be in the same situation again. You could meet someone who will offer financial assistance.

DOWNSIDE: You could find yourself with loans you cannot repay. A period of financial insecurity lies ahead.

30-SECOND READING

Jermaine has no idea what he wants to do when he grows up. He is getting worried because a lot of his friends seem to know what direction they want to head in. This card is saying that there is no need to make a decision now. He should work hard at school and take time to explore as many options as possible until he finds something that really excites him.

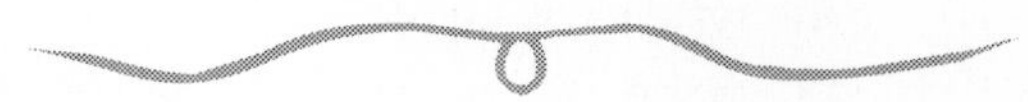

SEVEN OF PENTACLES

In this card we see a man resting awhile and looking intently at seven pentacles, or material things. It looks as if he has worked hard for the plants, but now it is time for nature to work its magic. In other words, some things are out of our hands. All we can do is our best, and then we have to simply wait and see.

Questions to ask yourself if you draw the Seven of Pentacles:

- Are you taking stock of your life so far?
- Are you waiting to hear from someone or about something?
- Are you ready to reap what you sow?
- What do you need to let go of?
- What is growing through hard work?

Friends

UPSIDE: You are beginning to understand that friendship requires commitment and a lot of give and take, but any personal sacrifices you have to make are well worth it. Friendship doesn't just happen. You have to work at it.

DOWNSIDE: This card suggests gossip and friends who are untrustworthy.

KEY THOUGHTS: Whatever you have worked at (including a relationship between people) has reached a point at which it can grow by itself. Step back from it for a while and congratulate yourself. Keep calm and promise yourself a good rest. All will be well—but only after that rest.

School

UPSIDE: You are anxious about some exam results. If you know you did your best, rest easy; the results will be fine.

DOWNSIDE: You reap what you sow. If you didn't work hard for your exams, you can't expect to pass with flying colors.

Dating

UPSIDE: You could do with a little more action. If you want to meet someone new, make the effort to meet new people.

DOWNSIDE: Don't sacrifice your integrity to get a date. It isn't worth it.

Family

UPSIDE: A lot of changes ahead for your family. Some of them won't be easy, but it will all turn out well in the end.

DOWNSIDE: Certain family members need to think things through before taking action.

Interests

UPSIDE: This is the card of steady progress rather than a quick rise to the top. You may be drawn to a life of learning or teaching.

DOWNSIDE: Poor planning and disorganization can ruin your chances.

Health/Looks

UPSIDE: You feel satisfied with yourself. Perhaps you have lost some weight recently or improved your fitness levels or have a haircut that looks terrific.

DOWNSIDE: A certain amount of anxiety and unease about your appearance.

Money

UPSIDE: Through hard work and effort, you will see financial reward.

DOWNSIDE: This is not a good time to make decisions about money.

30-SECOND READING

Monica would like to help her mom, who is having a hard time making ends meet. The card is saying that there are a lot of practical chores around the house that Monica could apply herself to. If she focused on doing them well, it would take some of the burden off her mom's shoulders.

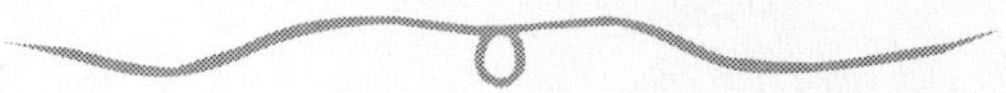

EIGHT OF PENTACLES

The Eight of Pentacles has a simple message: practice makes perfect. We see an artist working patiently on a project with great pride and skill. He is absorbed in his task. The Eight of Pentacles shows the training that brings discipline and skill. Any kind of work, be it academic or artistic or emotional, will fail if it is done only for the end result. You have to care about the work itself.

Questions to ask yourself if you draw the Eight of Pentacles:

- What are you working on?
- Do you care about the work that you do?

- Are you setting a good example for others?
- What new skill are you learning?
- What are you perfecting?

Friends

UPSIDE: Friends are important to you, but so is your schoolwork. You have the balance right.
DOWNSIDE: Your friends are charming but insincere, and you feel disillusioned and unhappy.

School

UPSIDE: The care and attention you put into your work is admirable. Your teachers have noticed.
DOWNSIDE: Put more care and attention into your work. It will be worth the effort.

Dating

UPSIDE: A new relationship is on the way.
DOWNSIDE: If you aren't willing to be open and honest with potential partners, your relationship will never get beyond the superficial.

Family

UPSIDE: A member of your family may receive a long-deserved promotion or recognition of some kind.
DOWNSIDE: You feel disillusioned and unhappy at home. Remember, your parents or guardians are only human. They will make mistakes, just like you do.

Interests

UPSIDE: It is possible that a hobby or creative talent can be turned into a profitable moneymaking scheme. You are rapidly picking up new talents and skills that will help you in your future career. You could be drawn to farming, gardening, athletics, dance, architecture, or the beauty/fashion business.

DOWNSIDE: Stop defining yourself by your interests. You are a human being, not a human doing.

Health/Looks

UPSIDE: You are blossoming into something quite remarkable.

DOWNSIDE: If you don't feel happy on the inside, you won't look happy on the outside.

Money

UPSIDE: Through hard work and effort, you will see financial reward.

DOWNSIDE: Don't make any hasty decisions about money.

KEY THOUGHTS:

This is a card suggesting effort and hard work, or a period of training. Love the work that you do, enjoy your studies, but don't forget about the outside world. Make sure you always give yourself some quality time. If possible, plan your day so you can balance work, leisure, and rest.

30-SECOND READING

Heidi would like to go to a few concerts but has no money. What can she do? This card is saying that she ought to work hard at home and in the community and save as much as she can. This won't be easy, but slowly her savings will increase and she will be able to finance her leisure activities.

NINE OF PENTACLES

In the Nine of Pentacles we see an elegantly dressed woman standing in a flourishing garden, with a hooded bird on her gloved hand. Material security has been established, and she is enjoying what she has achieved. You will notice that the woman is by herself, which suggests she has had to make certain sacrifices to get to where she is in life. The card indicates success, but not merely material success; it also means the sense of certainty that comes with knowing you have made the right choices. The pentacles growing on the bushes symbolize a life that is productive and alive. Questions to ask yourself:

- Are you enjoying your success?
- Do you enjoy your own company?
- What are you achieving through hard work?
- What are you sacrificing for success?
- Is it time to reward yourself for your efforts?

Friends

UPSIDE: Your friends have nothing but respect and admiration for you. Enjoy it.

DOWNSIDE: Certain friends are dragging you down. You don't need them in your life.

School

UPSIDE: You are receiving praise for your work, and you deserve it.

DOWNSIDE: Too much time spent in leisure is affecting your schoolwork.

Dating

UPSIDE: When you do enter into a relationship it will be a very happy one.

DOWNSIDE: How much effort are you putting into this dating thing? Remember that you reap what you sow.

Family

UPSIDE: After a period of uncertainty, things are settling down again into a comfortable routine.

DOWNSIDE: It isn't wise for your family to make big purchases, especially household items or new furniture.

Interests

UPSIDE: It might be time to start looking outside your comfort zone for new challenges.
DOWNSIDE: You aren't really challenging yourself at the moment.

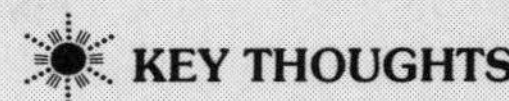

KEY THOUGHTS:
Work hard and reap the benefits of what you sow. Decide what you want and what matters to you, and channel your energy into that. Embrace and anticipate change. See it as a challenge; an opportunity for further development.

Health/Looks

UPSIDE: Elegance and charm are your trademark.
DOWNSIDE: Lack of discipline as far as diet, exercise, and healthy living are concerned will take its toll on your looks.

Money

UPSIDE: Money and success are around the corner.
DOWNSIDE: Gambles will not pay off.

30-SECOND READING
Carl is due to leave school in one month's time, and he feels sad. What can he do to stop feeling this way? This card is saying that he has achieved a lot socially and academically. He should sit back and enjoy his successes. There is still a month left to enjoy, and he should not waste a minute of it feeling sad.

TEN OF PENTACLES

A man and woman stand under an archway leading to a family garden. A child stands with them looking at two dogs, who attend to an old man. The Ten of Pentacles is one of the most mystical and deeply symbolic Minor Arcana cards. On the surface it seems to suggest happy home life, but the people seem to be taking their comfort for granted, and there doesn't seem to be much communication going on. The card appears mundane, but there are magic signs all over it—most noticeably the Hebrew tree of life. Notice also the magic wand, the scales, the old man. All these hidden signs highlight the basic meaning of the pentacles: The everyday world has a magic far greater than any of us usually see.

Questions to ask yourself if you draw the Ten of Pentacles:

- Do you see the magic in your life?
- Are you paying attention to what is going on around you?
- Is there an elderly member of your family who needs special care?
- What traditions or values are you questioning?
- Are you communicating with your loved ones about what is important to you?

Friends

UPSIDE: This is a period of contentment.

DOWNSIDE: You may be feeling bored with your current circle of friends.

School

UPSIDE: You are working hard on an exam or project. Your hard work will pay off.

DOWNSIDE: You are rejecting lots of school rules. You won't achieve anything by being disruptive.

Dating

UPSIDE: A good time for a relationship, as long as you communicate well with potential partners.

DOWNSIDE: You aren't letting potential partners know what you really think and feel, and this will cause problems in the long run.

Family

UPSIDE: Family comforts and the happiness of family gatherings are indicated.

DOWNSIDE: Poor communication creates a feeling of unease at home.

Interests

UPSIDE: Now is a good time for anything to do with travel, sport, and movement.

DOWNSIDE: You feel restricted in some way.

Health/Looks

UPSIDE: You feel good about yourself, and have every reason to.

DOWNSIDE: You lack confidence and self-belief.

Money

UPSIDE: Inheritances or gifts of money may occur.

DOWNSIDE: Lack of money or financial security is creating unease.

KEY THOUGHTS:

You can raise your level of achievement to whatever level you decide, regardless of where you are now. Many of the world's brightest people were slow starters. Thomas Edison, who invented not only the light bulb and phonograph but also many other things we rely on, was expelled from school for being a slow learner. All you need to do is believe in yourself and the magic that is all around you—at home, at school, in your friends, in nature, and in the very fact that life exists.

30-SECOND READING

Sharon is feeling bored and restless at home and longs to make her own way in the world. This card tells her that she would see magic and excitement all around her if she would look deeply into her own life. She doesn't need to leave home to find excitement. One day she will look back and realize just how special these last few years at home really were.

11 Your Kingdom Awaits:

The Sixteen Royalty Cards

In this chapter we will complete our journey of the Minor Arcana and meet the sixteen Royalty cards, also called Court cards. Every suit of the Minor Arcana has a royal household with a Page, Knight, Queen, and King. You'll notice that the format for these cards is a little different from the others. This is because the Court cards represent you or someone you know or want to get to know. They can represent people who will influence your life in some way, or they can symbolize qualities within yourself that you need to develop. As you glance through the cards, see if you can match them to various roles you play in life, or to various people in your life. To help you do this, here is a list of occupations and interests the Court cards can represent:

Wands: Teachers, inventors, politicians, salespeople, leaders, managers, administrators, innovators, competitors.

Cups: Psychiatrists, social workers, artists, musicians, psychics, counselors.

Swords: Scientists, mathematicians, researchers, engineers, writers, lawyers, computer consultants, travel agents, secret service, detectives, thinkers.

Pentacles: Doctors, dentists, students, builders, farmers, gardeners, beauticians, athletes, dancers, gamblers.

The Court cards also represent certain behavior patterns. The Pages typically suggest energy, curiosity, innocence, enthusiasm, and optimism. The Knights are a symbol of enthusiasm, action, training, and service. The Queens and Kings stand for mastery and self-discipline and devotion to others. You can relate the cards to stages in your life as well. The ones of particular interest to you right now will be the Pages and Knights. A Page often signifies a young adult. A Knight usually represents someone who is taking their first steps out in the world, or anyone who is learning through studying or doing. Queens and Kings are generally thought to represent older people, but they also signify younger people who are wise beyond their years or who have a level of responsibility beyond their years. They can also represent parents, guardians, teachers, mentors, or guides.

A King, Knight, or Page does not always literally represent a man, and a Queen does not always literally represent a woman. The cards can sometimes indicate the sex of a person who is influencing your life, but more often they show qualities or attitudes associated with these figures that might be good for you to develop. If a girl gets a male card, it suggests that she needs to work on the qualities associated with that card. The same is true if a boy gets a female card. The development of characteristics traditionally associated with the opposite sex will help you become a more complete person.

Finally, don't forget that your response to each card matters a great deal. The Court cards can offer great insights into your life, relationships, and personality. Think about what each card means to you. What or who does the figure on the card remind you of? What stage of life is each card in? What personality traits are suggested? What card do you identify with and why? Is the card about you, someone you know, or someone you would like to get to know?

Now, if you are ready, let's meet the royal family.

THE HOUSE OF WANDS

PAGE OF WANDS

The Page is standing by some pyramids, symbolic of wisdom. He looks up at his wand, suggesting that he is looking for inspiration. The Pages often symbolize beginnings or study. It's rather like the way you felt when you started your new school, college, or first job. This is the card of true friendship, representing a person who will stand by you no matter what. It can also be seen as a restless, energetic, enthusiastic young person, or a faithless friend. Perhaps you may feel restless yourself for no particular reason. You may have a flash of inspiration and creativity, which you should pursue, because success is likely. Confusion, anxiety, and false starts can be a problem, and the Page needs to find the maturity to deal with this.

KEY THOUGHTS:

This is a period of exciting new opportunities. You need to invest time and energy if these possibilities are to lead to success. You feel excited but restless about the changes that lie ahead. Keep your cool, take time to plan and think, and remember you are creating your life.

Questions to ask yourself if you draw the Page of Wands:

- Are you looking for inspiration?
- Are you being told that you show great promise?

- What are you getting excited about?
- Are you curious, or resistant to learning?

30-SECOND READING

Barbara has decided she wants to leave home as soon as she passes her final exams. This card tells Barbara that her need for independence is good, but before she takes any action she needs to really think about how she will earn money and take care of herself. Barbara needs to be a little less impulsive and more practical about her decision to leave home.

KNIGHT OF WANDS

The Knight carries a wand and rides a high-spirited horse. The Knight has taken the inspiration of the Page and is using it in his life. This Knight is the card of action, adventure, and risk-taking. Unlike the Page, the Knight is moving quickly on a horse, which shows that the adventure has started. You will notice the primary colors of this card, which show the rawness and brightness of the experiences enjoyed. Fire symbolizes movement, and here we see that quality in the extreme. This guy loves to be where the action is, but he needs a sense of purpose and direction if his adventure is to end successfully. Without direction, the Knight represents confusion, disrupted projects, and disharmony. The card can represent a energetic quality within yourself, or someone you know with an impulsive personality.

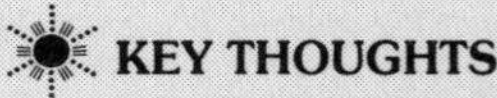

KEY THOUGHTS:

You will be inspired to do something adventurous and new. This is an incredibly exciting time for you. Enjoy the feeling, but keep your feet firmly on the ground. Success can be yours if you build the right foundations by creating genuine goals, keeping your energy levels high with positive thinking, and surrounding yourself with people who will support and encourage you.

Questions to ask yourself if you draw the Knight of Wands:

- Are you starting a new adventure?
- What are you fired up about?
- Are you fighting a battle?
- What are you trying to prove?

30-SECOND READING

Kim is bored. This card shows either that soon she will meet someone who will encourage her to experience new things, or that she needs to rediscover the spirit of adventure within herself. Kim has been thinking about taking a year off from her studies to do volunteer work abroad, and this card indicates that it might be just what she needs at this stage in her life.

QUEEN OF WANDS

The Queen of Wands sits holding symbols of her authority and status. She looks confident and intends to rule with love and understanding. This card can often signify an older woman, like a mother, for example, but it also suggests the ability to draw good things to you with a confident, optimistic frame of mind. Sometimes when a person seems to love life, the world responds by sending that person good things. The Queen represents the kind of person you want to have around in a crisis. She is warm-natured and a good organizer. She is always calm and loving and offers advice and emotional assistance without wanting anything in return. Is this you, or are you looking for someone to support you through a tough time? There is a warning here, though. If too many problems are heaped upon her, the Queen may lose her optimism and become angry and bitter. You can only push people so far.

KEY THOUGHTS:

This card shows that you need to inject more confidence and optimism into your life. It will make all the difference. A positive attitude will help create positive results. When negative thoughts appear, brush them aside and replace them with positive ones. You can't afford the luxury of self-doubt.

Questions to ask yourself if you draw the Queen of Wands:

- Are your leadership skills being called upon?
- Are you proud of yourself?
- Are you a positive thinker?
- Is a woman inspiring you?

30-SECOND READING

Dan is feeling a little down. He didn't do well in his exams, didn't get the job he wanted, and he feels too ashamed to

(continued)

tell his girlfriend how he feels. This card shows that Dan really needs someone he can open his heart to. Perhaps he should talk to his girlfriend, but if he can't do that he needs to think about what can be done to turn things around. Perhaps he could work harder at school, and apply for another job.

KING OF WANDS

Facing sideways, the King holds a wand. He looks as if he is deep in thought. The King indicates a strong-willed person. This is a man who gets results. He believes he is right, and it is natural for other people to follow him. At the same time, we see that he looks a little uncomfortable in his role, as if he would like to leap up and try something new. The King is powerful and commanding, but there is a danger that he can become a little intolerant. You may have to guard against that yourself, or perhaps you know someone who is impatient with you in some way. The King's task is to learn to combine discipline and authority with understanding and respect for others. If he doesn't do this, he can become deceitful and selfish.

KEY THOUGHTS:

Have the courage of your convictions. If you want to succeed, you have to be strong like the King and believe in yourself. Self-belief will require a level of maturity and responsibility, but if you are serious about succeeding in life, you will find it.

Questions to ask yourself if you draw the King of Wands:

- Is someone treating you harshly?
- Are you been harsh toward someone?
- Are you in a leadership role?
- Is a man inspiring you?

30-SECOND READING
David is worried about his little brother, who he thinks is being bullied. This card suggests that David isn't the one who can help right now. His brother needs to talk to an adult who can help and support him through this difficult time. David decides not to talk to his brother, but to talk to his parents instead. He discovers that his parents are aware of the situation and have been in touch with the school.

THE HOUSE OF CUPS

PAGE OF CUPS

The Page in this picture contemplates a fish. A fish is a symbol of fertility and new beginnings. The Page of Cups indicates creative potential waiting to be realized. You may discover a new talent or embark on a new course of study. This card also indicates that you must love yourself before you can love others. A person represented by this card will be kind, loving, and in a position to help in some way—or it could mean that you are a sensitive and artistic person who is emotionally vulnerable and in need of affection. The danger here is having an overactive imagination and living in a dream world.

KEY THOUGHTS:

Your creative potential is waiting to be realized. You will find ways to rise above hurt and disappointment. Life isn't easy, it isn't fair, and it isn't right, but that's the way it is. You can either moan about your problems or solve them. It's in the whole process of meeting and solving problems that life has its meaning. The only way to grow is to be challenged. It is through the pain of confronting and resolving problems that we learn and grow. Problems bring pain and frustration, but they also create courage, joy, and wisdom.

Questions to ask yourself if you draw the Page of Cups:

- Are your emotions running wild?
- Are you in emotional pain?
- Are you living in a dream world?
- Do you want to be carefree?

30-SECOND READING

Steve is a great computer game fan. This card appears in a reading, and it warns him that he spends too much time in a dream world and not enough time in the real world. There is nothing wrong with his love for computer games; he just needs to make sure that he gets some action in the world outside, too.

KNIGHT OF CUPS

This graceful—not warlike—Knight holds a cup in his hand. His winged helmet suggests that his imagination is taking flight. Dreams dominate this card, with a Knight lost in his imaginings, but it is important to remember that he is a Knight, and Knights aren't about dreaming. Knights are about doing, and this one needs to rouse himself into action. This card suggests that news is on the horizon. Romance could be in the air, and you may fall in love with someone who is sensitive, idealistic, and imaginative. Alternatively, you may find those characteristics within yourself. On the downside, you need to avoid someone who is a heartbreaker and doesn't have your best interests at heart. This card can represent someone (perhaps you or someone you know) who does not wish to commit himself or herself.

KEY THOUGHTS:

Imagination can help you visualize the potential that lies within you, but to be effective, imagination needs to be followed by action. It's good to think about what you could do or what you could be. It's good to dream about the endless possibilities before you. But you also need to ensure that your active imagination produces something in the real world. Never stop dreaming, but make sure you balance your dreaming with doing.

Questions to ask yourself if you draw the Knight of Cups:

- Are you looking for something or someone?
- What are you dreaming about?
- Are you willing to commit yourself to a course of action?
- Are you caring too much for others and not enough for yourself?

30-SECOND READING

Ron's girlfriend recently left him. His friends are telling him to forget about her. Ron knows that the relationship wasn't right, but he is finding it hard to move on. The card is telling him that he has felt the pain long enough. The time has come to let the pain go and start dating and having fun again.

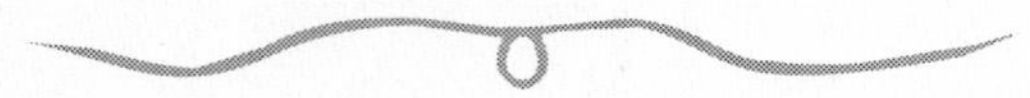

QUEEN OF CUPS

The Queen of Cups sits at the seashore contemplating the future. She is a dreamer and may possess psychic ability. Her loving nature and sensitivity to others makes her a wonderful friend. If you drew this card it suggests that you need to develop a better relationship with yourself. There may be a tendency to become self-absorbed, but this can be avoided by ensuring you stay loyal and devoted to those you care about. The Queen is the most successful and balanced of the suit of Cups and maybe even of all the Minor Arcana. She blends imagination with action, and sensitivity with usefulness. We could all benefit from her loving intelligence and joyful vision of life.

KEY THOUGHTS:

Become your own best friend, and your self-esteem will immediately improve. Imagine that you have stepped out of your body and that you are standing next to yourself (don't think too much about this; use your imagination). Now look at your other self. What would you say to him or her that is comforting and helpful? How would you encourage this person to feel more confident about himself or herself? Talk to yourself the way you would to your best friend.

Questions to ask yourself if you draw the Queen of Cups:

- Are you living your dreams?
- Are you in control of your feelings, or do they control you?
- Are you loving yourself enough?
- Do you find it easy to understand other people?

30-SECOND READING

Louisa wants to know if she will ever be famous. The card is saying that whatever path she chooses in life, she will do well as long as she combines intelligence with action, pays attention to her feelings, and takes good care of herself. She should concentrate less on being famous and more on loving the work that she chooses.

KING OF CUPS

Here we see a King riding the tides of life. This man is the captain of his own ship, or life. Whether the seas are rough or calm, the wise and imaginative King is full of creative possibilities. This card suggests that you may get some good advice, possibly from a teacher or

counselor, or you may give some good advice to someone yourself. It may also represent a part of you that needs to be developed. You might need to learn to be more open and trust your feelings. On the downside, this card can suggest a person who is very secretive, dishonest, and hot-tempered, who can give the wrong impression. I hope this isn't you. Like the King of Wands, this man does not look that comfortable. He does not look at the cup he holds. This card reminds you of the importance of appreciating the many good things in your life.

KEY THOUGHTS:

Don't hide your emotions. Find ways to express them. Learn to accept and manage your feelings. It really is okay to feel angry, jealous, selfish, sad, and afraid—and all of those other emotions you may think of as bad. Acknowledge and experience your feelings, and then let them go. That way, your self-esteem will remain intact.

Questions to ask yourself if you draw the King of Cups:

- Do you love your life?
- Do you feel in control?
- Is something or someone upsetting you?
- Are you being honest with yourself?

30-SECOND READING

Bella is anxious about her weight. This card tells her that she needs to be more open about how she feels. She needs to talk to friends and family instead of bottling up her worries and fears.

THE HOUSE OF SWORDS

PAGE OF SWORDS

The Page walks quickly holding his sword, the symbol of mental clarity. He is learning how to make the best choices he can, and is willing to take responsibility for and learn from what results. You will also notice that the sword is upright. Sometimes it is good to be detached and rise above problems so that things can be seen in perspective. At other times detachment isn't so good if problems that need to be worked through aren't solved, resulting in indecisiveness. Remember that the Pages, like the other Court cards, represent actual people you may meet, or emotional states within yourself. This card represents a quick-witted, intelligent, and independent-minded person. He is eager to learn and good at turning things to his advantage. Is this you or someone you know?

KEY THOUGHTS:

If there is something you want to do, set your goals and do the best that you can. If things work out, great. If they don't work out, acknowledge that things didn't go according to plan and then detach yourself from the situation. Let yourself off the hook. We all make mistakes. Learn from them, and then move on.

Questions to ask yourself if you draw the Page of Swords:

- Are you learning from your mistakes, or dwelling on them?
- Whom or what are you detaching yourself from?

- Are you cutting yourself off from things?
- Where might you be more decisive?

30-SECOND READING

Josh is fed up with hearing his parents argue. At first he tried to make sense of it all, but now he has learned to detach himself from the situation. This card is telling him that he has made the best decision as far as his parents are concerned, but detachment isn't an approach that he should keep using. There will be times in his life when it is important for him to express his feelings and get involved.

KNIGHT OF SWORDS

With his sword drawn, the Knight races at full speed into battle. The card can indicate a sudden or impulsive need to make a change of some sort, like ending a relationship or dropping a subject at school. It also carries a warning against being impulsive, because impulsiveness can cause havoc. It suggests that problems need to be faced head-on. The Knight of Swords may also represent a good friend who will help you through your difficulties. The Knights do tend to characterize youthful go-getters full of energy and eager to seek out new adventures, but they can also be the type of people who breeze into your life and just as swiftly breeze out. The Knight of

Swords is perhaps the most fast-moving and easily bored of the Knights, so if this card is drawn, a quieter, more careful approach may be required.

 **KEY THOUGHTS:**

Develop an action plan before you leap into action. It might help to write down your plan. When you commit on paper, you take yourself much more seriously. Sometimes the plan won't work and you'll need to make changes, but that doesn't matter. Planning will increase your chances of success, keep you from making hasty decisions, and demonstrate to you that you really can create your reality. That's a great feeling.

Questions to ask yourself if you draw the Knight of Swords:

- Are you fighting for a cause?
- Are you impulsive and headstrong?
- Is there something you are eager to do or get involved in?
- Are you full of energy?

30-SECOND READING

Kira often acts on impulse. This card says that her wild behavior could cause problems. She is brave and strong, but she has to learn that there are limits. If she can check her impulsive behavior and think a little more before she acts, she can transform her courage and readiness to face problems into a strength, not a weakness.

QUEEN OF SWORDS

The Queen on this card faces sideways with her sword upright and her right hand extended in greeting. This woman is graceful, fair-minded, independent, and determined. She is cool in a crisis and should never be underestimated. Despite her strength and intelligence, she sometimes feels cut off and alone. Her cool, quick-thinking mind is her strength, but she can also be intolerant and judgmental. This may be someone you know, or it could mean that you need to drop your defenses a little and allow other people to help you when you are in need. All of the Queens are mature and self-possessed, but the Queen of Swords is the one that symbolizes the wisdom and maturity that come through experiencing pain, loss, setbacks, and disappointments with courage and honesty.

KEY THOUGHTS:

Impossibly high standards can keep others at a distance. Be more gentle to yourself and others. Always try your best, but accept that you will make mistakes and have off days.

Questions to ask yourself if you draw the Queen of Swords:

- Are you cool toward others?
- What is your mind set on doing?

- Are you intolerant sometimes?
- Is a highly motivated and independent person influencing you?

30-SECOND READING

Errol does not get along with his mother. This card agrees that his mother can sometimes be distant. There is little he can do but hope that she will open her eyes and her arms to him. He isn't doing anything wrong and needs to understand that this is his mother's problem, not his. The card also expresses sorrow for his mother and the loving relationship she is missing out on.

KING OF SWORDS

The King of Swords is a little similar to the Justice card in the Major Arcana. The King holds a sword in his right hand, suggesting that he has power over life and death. This King sets aside his personal beliefs and bases his advice and judgments on the truth. This is the card of authority, power, judgment, intelligence, and ethics. This man likes to be in a position of authority and is independent by nature. Do you recognize yourself or someone you know here? The King has learned to control his emotions and deal with situations in a logical, rational way. The danger here is arrogance, prejudice, and a need for power. There is a fine line between the power of judgment and power for its own sake.

 **KEY THOUGHTS:**

Look at things from a different perspective. If you are convinced that you can't do something, remember that there was a time when everyone was convinced that the Earth was flat. Whenever you catch yourself thinking negatively, pause, take a deep breath, and change the thought to something more positive—so that "I can't" becomes "I'll try," or "I'm no good" becomes "I could be good."

Questions to ask yourself if you draw the King of Swords:

- Are you the peacemaker?
- Are you passing judgment on someone or something?
- What laws do you live by?
- What will you or won't you tolerate?

30-SECOND READING

Julie wants to know if she will have children. The card is saying that she probably will, but should aim for balance in her life and have other goals, too. Much depends on the choices she makes over the next decade or two in her life, and whether or not her commitment to having children remains the same.

HOUSE OF PENTACLES

PAGE OF PENTACLES

The Page stands in nature intently staring at a pentacle, symbol of the material world. This card suggests that if you are patient and hard-working you will make steady progress and see your efforts pay off. You may be embarking on a new course of study, or applying for a job. You could meet someone who is practical and reliable and whose love of learning encourages you to apply yourself a little more. This is the card of study, research, and a desire for knowledge. Good news is suggested. There may even be extra money coming in. On the downside, this card warns against a rebellious, demanding person or a tendency in you to be unreliable.

KEY THOUGHTS:

Care less for the rewards or social position and more for the work itself. Learn to focus all your attention on the task at hand instead of worrying about the future or regretting the past. Learn to "be" as well as learning to "do." Spend a few moments each day in silence. Turn off the television and radio. Don't do anything; sit in peace, listen to your breathing, and just be.

Questions to ask yourself if you draw the Page of Pentacles:

- Are you receiving a scholarship or financial assistance for school?
- Are you studying hard?

- Are you starting a new course to enhance your career prospects?
- Are you feeling fit and healthy?

30-SECOND READING

Sue is being encouraged by her dance teacher to audition for dance school. This card suggests that Sue's dance teacher is a positive influence who can help Sue achieve success. Before Sue decides to audition, she needs to commit herself to an intensive training period that can help her determine whether or not to dedicate herself to a career in dance.

KNIGHT OF PENTACLES

Riding a horse, the Knight holds a pentacle in his hand. The image suggests a conventional, practical young man who leaves nothing to chance. He accepts responsibility easily and is hardworking and trustworthy. The downside of all this is that his static personality makes him a little dull! (I'm sure this isn't you.) This is the card of slow but steady progress. It may not seem as if you are getting very far, but if you are patient you will reach your goal. Life may seem boring sometimes, but efforts will be rewarded in the future. This card could also mean that someone who is dependable, responsible, and hardworking may enter your life and help you when you need it.

KEY THOUGHTS:

Discover the real source of your strength, within yourself and in life. Are you being honest with yourself? Sometimes we are not entirely true to ourselves. Are you doing things because you feel you should, even though it doesn't feel right to you? Are you afraid of saying no? Are you trying to please someone? What is it that you want to do? If you live a lie you won't find happiness. Be true to yourself, and happiness is yours for the taking.

Questions to ask yourself if you draw the Knight of Pentacles:

- What are you working hard for?
- Do you pay attention to detail?
- Do you work hard, or are you a slacker?
- Are you looking for work?

30-SECOND READING

Jay is doing a lot of baby-sitting for his little brother. His little brother now tries to follow him around everywhere. This card indicates the responsibility Jay has, but it also shows that Jay is proud of his ability to care for his brother. Sometimes Jay finds it all a bit much, but he knows that in years to come he will look back and feel proud of what he did and how it prepared him to be a father, should he have children.

QUEEN OF PENTACLES

The Queen sits in a beautiful garden looking at a pentacle. She is a loving, nurturing woman who is capable and self-reliant. She is hard-working and enjoys the comforts of life. She can be materialistic, but she is also generous to others. This card suggests that there may be a chance to achieve something of real value, or you may meet someone who can help you achieve your goals. The card also warns against a possessive or mistrustful person. Generally, though, the Queen of Pentacles is a generous woman who may offer you emotional support or contacts or money, or help you find a way to earn money. Her self-sufficiency and optimism are admirable. This card is also suggesting the emergence of these qualities in yourself.

KEY THOUGHTS:

Look to your strengths. What are you good at? These things can be big or small, it does not matter which. Build yourself up. You may have weaknesses—everyone does—but you can change for the better. Forget false modesty. Look to your strengths. Trust in yourself and in the magic of your life.

Questions to ask yourself if you draw the Queen of Pentacles:

- Are you a person who likes to take care of or mother other people?
- Do you feel mothered?
- Are you content at home?
- Are you generous?

30-SECOND READING

Georgina has just become a teenage mom. How will it go? This card is positive. Georgina will find the experience harder than she could imagine, and there will be times when she wishes that she had waited until she was older with more knowledge of the world, but the relationship she creates with her child will be a fulfilling and happy one.

KING OF PENTACLES

Sitting peacefully in a garden, the King of Pentacles wears a robe symbolizing his wealth and status. This card indicates a loyal, good-natured man who is hardworking and practical. It bodes well for any financial situation. If this card appears in a reading, you may meet someone with these qualities, someone who is good with money and can advise you well. But this card is also suggesting that you adopt these qualities yourself. On the downside, it warns against someone who is untrustworthy, spiteful, and vicious.

KEY THOUGHTS:

There is great joy to be found in ordinary things. Responsibility and hard work are not burdens. They can bring you the success and happiness you deserve. Are you taking steps toward making your dreams come true? If not, why not? Don't become one of those adults you

(continued)

know who always complains that they never got what they wanted in life. Reach for the stars, be courageous, and start creating your life. Even if the steps you take are small ones, the important thing is that your journey begins.

Questions to ask yourself if you draw the King of Pentacles:

- Are you a responsible person?
- How well do you handle money?
- Do you need to be more practical?
- Are you too materialistic?

30-SECOND READING

Liam is worried about how he will pay for his college education. He asks the cards for advice. The King of Pentacles indicates that Liam has the ability to generate income, but he needs to do this through hard work rather than chance. In other words, he can't sit around hoping for money to fall into his lap; he has to find ways to earn it.

12

The Cards Most Likely to Send Shivers Down Your Spine

You have already come far enough in this book to know that no card in the Tarot deck is completely negative. You can always find something positive to focus on. But just to reassure you, let's look at the ones most likely to send shivers down your spine.

Death

Death is the card you probably fear the most, but as we stressed before, it doesn't usually mean an actual death; it can mean the end of a situation or phase in life. Leaving school, losing touch with old friends, moving to a different house, ending a relationship, leaving home, or having to clear out your childhood toys all represent the "death" or end of something. Of course, you are going to feel sad about the loss of something you value, but the Tarot can help you work through difficult emotions, like sadness, loss, and disappointment, to get to something more positive.

The Tarot will stress that endings are very important for your life to move forward. Nature teaches us that the old has to die to let the new grow. It's the same in your life. You have to let go of certain things in order to explore new things. Don't be frightened by the prospect of things ending. Get excited about the new possibilities that lie ahead.

The Devil

The Devil has a dark side, and usually when it appears in readings it isn't good news. If you do get The Devil in a reading, remind yourself that it is only when you can recognize where you might be going wrong that you can decide to make changes and direct your energy in a positive rather than a negative way. Sometimes the only way to learn is to make mistakes.

The Tower

Don't panic. Instead, see The Tower as an early warning that if you don't do something about a situation, things will start to fall apart around you. On the other hand, you could think of it as the card telling you that your life needs a good shakeup or change of direction.

The Hanged Man

The Hanged Man looks pretty gruesome, but what it is really suggesting is that you need to take some time out from a tense situation. Chill out! Sometimes when you are up to your ears in something you can get very hotheaded, and do or say something you later regret. Take time out to cool down and think about things from a different perspective.

The Hierophant

The Hierophant looks quite severe—a bit like a teacher who is always on your case. But the truth is that sometimes criticism or advice can be very helpful—especially if it keeps you from getting badly hurt. Remember, a mom will sharply scold a toddler for running out on a road. When you get a little older you are grateful for the warning.

Three of Swords

No one likes being dumped or having a relationship end or having their heart broken, but it is better to know where you stand so you can move on and find someone or something much, much better.

Eight of Swords

This picture is all about feeling trapped and restricted. But how much of this is in your mind? Take a look at the woman in the picture. Is the situation that bad? Why doesn't she just use her legs and walk away?

Nine of Swords

The Nine of Swords is the card of worry, fear, and sleepless nights. The figure on the card is sitting up in bed worrying. Is the worrying you are doing achieving anything? Is it really all that bad?

Ten of Swords

Perhaps you just need a good cry. Remember, what does not kill us makes us stronger. Feel the pain, then move on to better things.

Five of Pentacles

No one likes the idea of being poor. But this card may not be about financial difficulties. It could be a warning that you are getting so wrapped up in your problems that you are missing out on the opportunities around you.

Whenever a card with a strong negative association appears, remember that you are only human. You may not understand it now, but what is happening to you may well be for a good reason. Perhaps failing your exams was the best thing that could happen to you, because it made you realize that if you want something better in life you have to work for it. Perhaps your partner cheating with your best friend made you realize that your relationship wasn't working, and that you deserve better.

However bad life gets, remember that the main difference between successful people and unsuccessful people is that unsuccessful people give up or lose self-belief when life doesn't go their way. The Tarot reminds you that if you have courage, believe in yourself, and learn from your mistakes, there is no doubt that you will find the happiness and success you deserve.

Fun Exercise

Remove the cards mentioned in this section from the Tarot pack, and spend a few moments concentrating on each. Try to find only the positive meaning of each card. This will help take away the unnecessary fear and keep you from freaking out whenever a so-called negative card appears in a reading. Remember, the more relaxed you are when problems and setbacks occur, the more likely you are to find a solution that pulls you through.

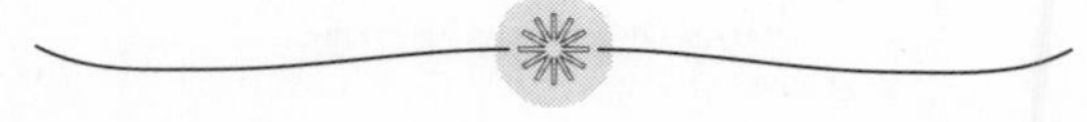

Part Three

Tarot Basics

✷ When you ask a question, the Tarot will reflect everything that revolves around that situation . . . the choice is always yours as to whether or not you follow the guidance offered.

—Annie Lionnet, *Secrets of Tarot*

13 Protecting Your Cards

Your Tarot pack is something very special, and it is important that you look after it well. Some people keep their cards wrapped in a silk scarf, while others keep them in a box or drawstring bag. It doesn't matter what you keep your cards in as long as you treat them with respect.

Far more important than the cards is the person who uses them. Treat yourself with respect, and it will be easy for you to treat your cards with respect. Don't use them when you are drunk, tired, upset, angry, or stressed. The time to use them is when you are in a calm frame of mind. The Tarot cards often appear at parties, where there is loud music in the background and lots of distraction. It can work in these situations, but only if the Tarot reader has his senses about him and is very familiar with the cards. When you are learning the Tarot, it's best to find a quiet environment where you can concentrate and reflect.

You will find that your friends will often ask you to read the cards for them. Don't fall into the trap of using the cards as a way to please your friends or raise your status. This may work in the short run, but in the long run you will feel exhausted and angry. If you spend your time running after other people, your own needs are not being met. It is important as a Tarot reader to learn to say no, because if you are giving lots of readings to please others, you're setting yourself up for exhaustion, which will limit the effectiveness of your readings.

When you are learning, you might find it difficult to give other people an effective reading, so it is best to do readings for yourself first until you get more confident. If you do give someone else a reading and have to refer to this book to find out the meanings of the cards, just explain that you are learning and need their help to learn. Most people will be happy to help out. When you get confident with the cards, you may find, as we did, that almost everyone you know wants you to do a reading for them. At this point you may even want to charge a small fee for your reading. Why? Because people value what they have to pay for, and therefore are more likely to concentrate. And you probably could use the extra cash!

Four big mistakes:

1. **The first mistake is boasting.**

   "I am really weird and far-out, man, much more interesting than you boring people."

   If all you want to do is use the Tarot to get attention from others, you are making a big mistake. Nobody will be impressed, and you will end up looking foolish.

2. **The second mistake is taking the cards too seriously.**

   "I can't take a bath right now—the cards aren't favorable."

   If you are consulting the Tarot about every little decision in your life, you are relying too heavily on it. All this shows is that you are refusing to take responsibility for your life. Remember, using the cards is all about you taking charge of your life and not letting other people or things, like the Tarot, make your choices for you.

3. **The third mistake is not treating the cards with respect.**
   "Let's do a Tarot reading at the party. It will be fun."
   Yes, there is a place for fun in life, but the Tarot is not a party trick. If you want the cards to help you, you have to make a serious effort to understand them and treat them with respect.

4. **The fourth mistake is being opinionated.**
   "I did a reading for you and this is what you should do . . ."
   This isn't the way to go. Nobody likes to be told what to do. You don't like it, so why should other people?

Mistakes one and four point out the danger of thinking too highly of yourself. There is a difference between self-esteem and arrogance. People with self-esteem are confident, but also respectful and interested in others. As a result, other people are more willing to help them get what they want. Arrogant people are only interested in themselves. Nobody wants to help them get what they want, so they rarely get it. Mistakes one and three are about lack of self-esteem, and we've already mentioned how damaging that can be.

Approach the cards with respect and understanding, and they will work their magic in your life. Listen to their advice, but at the end of the day remember that the cards are only giving you an opinion. You transform the magic of the cards into personal power when you take the information they give and have the courage to make your own choices.

Don't get overinvolved with the cards. The best Tarot card readers are those who have a balanced life. Never forget that your health, family, school, friends, and outside interests are more important. In fact, the more life experience you get, the better at Tarot reading you will become. Every time you gain a little more life experience, you will look at a card differently and become a better reader.

And finally, make sure the cards are used only by you—except, of course, when you ask someone to shuffle the cards before you do a reading for them. Other people should not be allowed to mess around with them, because then the cards wouldn't be personally yours anymore.

Fun Exercise

Look through the seventy-eight cards and choose five of them. They will reflect the current state of your home life, school life, family life, romantic life, and your hopes and dreams for the future. Take your time with this exercise; there is no hurry. Now look up the meanings of each card. Don't ignore your own thoughts about the meanings of the cards; your own impressions have just as much value as what you read. Now put the five cards in a circle. Look at them all. Do you get a sense of unhappiness, or do you get a sense of balance and happiness?

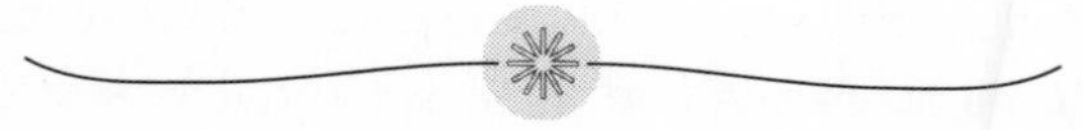

14 Asking Questions

It's always good to have a question in mind when you do a Tarot card reading, even if it is just a general one, although specific questions tend to make it easier for the cards to offer suggestions and options to you. It might be wise to first write down your question, or ask the person you are doing a reading for to write their question down. This will help you focus on the issue you want the cards to highlight. As you shuffle the cards (more on that later), really concentrate on the question.

The most important thing to realize about asking the Tarot questions is that, like anything in life, you get back what you put in. If you ask silly questions like "What haircut should I have?" you will get silly answers. If you ask too many questions at one reading the cards will give a confused answer, so focus on just one issue. If you constantly ask the same question, eventually the Tarot pack will not bother answering anymore. An example of this was Lori, who kept on asking when her boyfriend was going to stop chasing after other girls. Since she never bothered to challenge him about it in the real world, she became as much a part of the problem as he was. The cards gave her this advice on the first three readings, but then when she kept asking again and again they came back with The Fool. If she was not going to do something about the situation, why should they?

The key is to ask an open question that requires more than just a yes-or-no answer. The best questions start with *how, why, what,* and *might*. Because the Tarot only deals with possibilities, it is best not to begin with *should I, will I,* or *when*. You may think of life in terms of black and white, yes or no, right or wrong, but life isn't like that. There are good choices and bad choices, but everything has its upside and downside. For example, Tom decided to study hard for his high school diploma. This was a good choice, but it meant he had to sacrifice some, though not all, of his social time with friends. Toni spent all of her time hanging out with friends. This was a poor choice as she missed out on her education, but the upside was that she made some firm friendships.

The Tarot doesn't often give you a straight yes or no. This is because every path taken in life has an upside and a downside, and these need to be taken into consideration. Here are typical questions that the Tarot can handle:

- Why am I having such a hard time at school?
- How can my relationship with my parents improve?
- What can I do to improve my chances of happiness?
- Is it in my best interests to ask him or her out?
- What might I learn from this part-time job?

You need to be careful about health questions. The cards can give general advice, but it is always best to talk to your doctor about anything that concerns you. The Tarot also has no time for silly questions like these:

- Should I wear black or red shoes to the party?
- Will that new makeup make my skin look better?
- Has my friend had sex with his girlfriend?
- How can I get out of washing the car this Sunday?

If you are asking questions like these, come back to the cards when your life is a little more interesting!

And finally, remember at all times that the answers to your questions will come in the form of suggestions and the identification of new options. The whole point is to expand your point of view. You will get guidelines rather than advice. You need to carefully consider the suggestions and options represented by each card and then decide what rings true for you. Really, all you are doing is getting in touch with your own inner wisdom.

Asking Questions about Yourself

Yes, you can ask the Tarot questions about yourself. You don't have to read for other people or get other people to read for you. In fact, when you are learning to read the cards it is often best to start by practicing on yourself. Many Tarot readers regularly use the cards to think about various issues in their life, and you may find this works well for you. Sometimes, though, you may prefer to have someone else do a reading for you. This is because you often are so close to the issues that you can't see the forest for the trees. You no longer can step back from the situation and reflect on it in a calm, detached way. Think about it—isn't it always easier to see what is going wrong in a friend's life rather than in your own?

Look at it this way. Suppose you ask the cards about your chances of making the football team. You might pick the Knight of Swords, which means rushing headlong into things. You probably wouldn't connect this to the fact that you smoke. A skilled Tarot reader, however, might spot the nicotine stains on your teeth and warn you that you need to get the smoking situation sorted out, or you will be rushing headlong into disaster. In that case, the choice is yours. You know you are doing something that isn't good for your athletic career. It's up to you to make the decision to stop.

How Often Should You Use the Cards?

You can use the cards as often as you like. The more familiar you are with the cards, the more they will tell you. It isn't good to keep asking the same question every day, though. Wait at least a month after asking the first time before you ask again. As we have stressed, the important thing is the attitude with which you approach the cards. Use them as a learning tool, and they will give you insight into your life. Get too anxious about them, and they, like any good friend, will start to resent your dependence. Give your cards room to breathe, please.

15 Predicting Your Future

You may not realize it, but psychic power is not something that only some people have. The potential is there within all of us, including you.

- Do you sometimes think of someone a minute before they phone you?
- Do you sometimes look at someone when they aren't looking at you, and then they turn around and look?
- Do you sometimes know what other people are thinking?
- Do you pick up vibrations when you walk into a room?

If the answer is yes to any of these questions, this could be an indication of your unique psychic potential. It can take many years to train and develop psychic ability, but working with the Tarot is one of many methods you can use to awaken your psychic power. As you work with the cards you may, in time, find yourself relying more and more on those flashes of unexplained intuition for your personal development and success.

Though the cards can be used to predict your future, for now you need to concentrate on how the cards can help you understand your present. We often spend so much time worrying about the future that we forget that our present *creates* our future. Every day is the most important day of your life. Every day is a new beginning. Every day things happen that can drastically affect the rest of your life. Today could be the day you decide on your future career, meet someone who becomes a lifelong friend, or take up a new interest that will lead you in directions you've never dreamed of.

The best way to think of the Tarot is that it gives you helpful advice, rather like that of a wise friend. It doesn't create your future, but it can help make your future better. Don't make the mistake Joel did, and think that the Tarot's advice about the future is written in stone. Joel asked if he would become a professional basketball player. The Tarot answered with lots of encouraging cards but also warned Joel not to put all his eggs in one basket. A year down the road he wasn't making the progress he should, and he blamed the cards. The basic problem was that Joel had only listened to what he wanted to hear. He had ignored the advice about keeping other options open.

Anything is possible in life, particularly when you are a teenager and you have so much time ahead of you. Ignore all those people who tell you that your life is written in the stars, or that what will be will be. It's just not true. Your future is not created by something or someone else. Of course there are some things you can't change, like the parents you have, the background you are born into, or the color of your skin, but there are also many things that you *can* change. If this book teaches you anything, we hope it is this: *You create your own future by the choices you make in the present.*

Every day you are creating your future. Make positive choices right now, and you increase your chances of a positive future. Make negative choices, and you are unlikely to get what you want in the future. Success and happiness don't just happen to people. If you want to be happy and successful, you have to make it happen. The cards can help point you in the right direction, but at the end of the day it's up to you. You are the force. You have the power within you to rise above whatever may have been passed down to you. No matter how bad things get, you can create a new life for yourself.

To reach your goals in life you must seize the initiative. If you are feeling bad about not being asked out, don't just sit around and sulk. Do something about it! Find ways to meet people. Be friendly and try smiling. Ask them out. Let them know how great you are. In the same way, don't wait for the perfect job to fall into your lap. Go after it. Send out your resume, learn to network, do volunteer work for a while. If you are in a store and need assistance, don't wait for the salesperson to find you; find *them.* If someone is rude to you, control how you react. Don't let the other person make you feel bad.

As you work with the Tarot it will ask you over and over about taking responsibility for your life. Are you in the driver's seat of your life, or are you merely a passenger? Are you conducting your orchestra, or waiting for direction? Are you hoping for good things to happen, or making them happen? Are you waiting for someone else to make changes for you, or are you creating your future? The choice is yours.

16 Simple Tarot Spreads

There is no right way to lay out Tarot cards. Some people always use a particular spread—or way of laying out the cards—to interpret them. Others just pick cards at random. When you are learning it's a good idea to start with one particular spread, and then you can try out various others. The spreads we recommend in this book are a few of the most well-known and easy to lay out.

Dealing the Cards

When you are ready to read the cards, sit somewhere that's quiet and comfortable. You can kneel down on the floor or use a table to spread the cards on. Make sure the pack is face-down, and give the cards a good shuffle. Now cut the cards into three decks using your left hand (hand nearest to the heart). Then put the three decks together in any order. If you prefer to shuffle the cards another way, that's fine. Some people prefer to spread all the cards (face-down, of course) in front of them, and then randomly pick however many cards the spread requires.

Now you are ready to begin by laying out the first cards, from the top of the deck.

The Touchstone Spread

Using the touchstone spread is a great way to get to know the cards one at a time. *Touchstone* means a point of reference. Select one card at the beginning of each day, and use it as a reference point for the events ahead. Then at the end of the day reflect on what has happened.

Example: If you draw The Lovers, you may begin the day focusing on affairs of the heart. At school you write a romantic poem for your English assignment; the boy or girl you like smiles at you; you hear your favorite love song on the radio. At the end of the day you feel upbeat about your life and can remind yourself that The Lovers is a card that is also about having a good relationship with yourself.

The Three-Card Spread

This involves laying out three cards to represent your past, present, or future. The card you lay down first is your past, the card in the middle is the present, and the card you lay down last is your future.

Example: Say you pick the Nine of Swords for your past, Temperance for the present, and The Sun for the future. The Nine of Swords shows that the past has been anxious. Temperance reveals that the present is becoming easier. The Sun shows that happiness is in store—maybe a love affair or a vacation in the sun.

The Celtic Cross

The Celtic Cross is a little more complex. Shuffle the cards, and lay out six cards face-down in the shape of a cross, as in the illustration. Then put four cards face-down alongside it. The Celtic Cross spread is very good for answering specific questions. In the next chapter we'll give you an example of how this works.

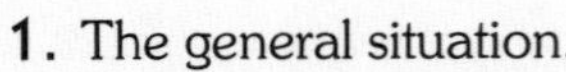

1. The general situation.
2. Obstacles in your path.
3. The past and the influence of the past on your question.
4. Influences working in your favor.
5. The near future.
6. The long-term future.
7. Yourself.
8. Home life.
9. Your hopes and fears.
10. Eventual outcome.

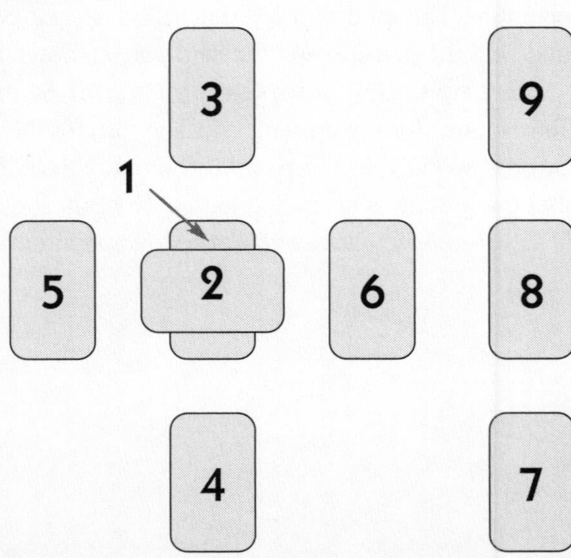

The Fifteen-Card Spread

This is great when you have plenty of time and really want to spend time looking and thinking about the cards you have drawn. Instead of one card each for your past, present, and future, you get five. You can use this spread for a general reading, or you can use it to address specific areas in your life, such as school, dating, family, and so on. Lay out five cards in a row, then five more cards above it and then five more cards again, as in the illustration below. Look at all five cards in each row, and see if you can work out what they are trying to say to you about your past, present, and future. What advice are you being given? What do you have to watch out for? What possibilities lie ahead?

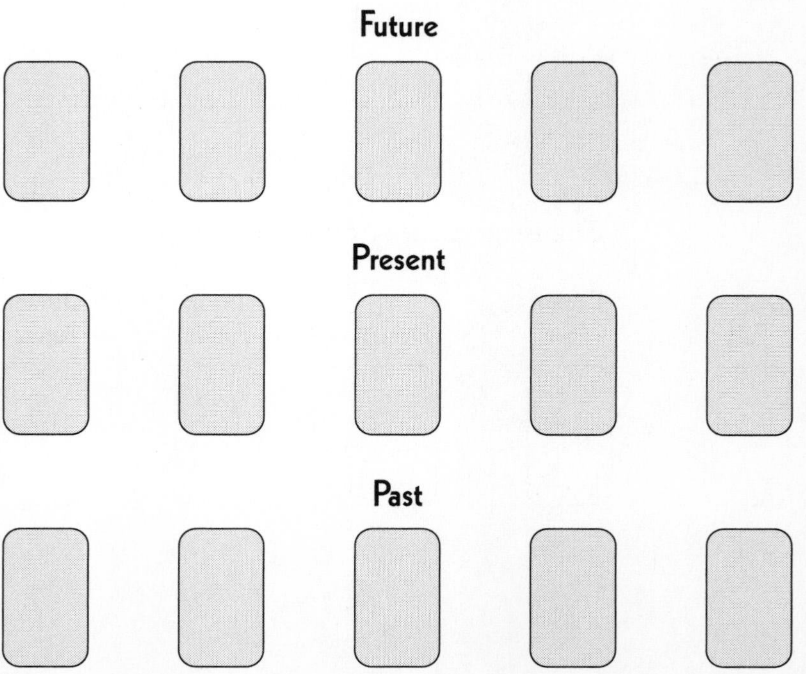

Specific-Issues Spread

The Celtic Cross, fifteen-card spread, touchstone spread, and three-card spread tend to be used for general readings. Sometimes, though, you may want to ask about a particular aspect of your life. It could be a relationship, school, work, a money or family issue, and so on. If this is the case, the specific-issues spread can be used.

The issue as the person you are reading for sees it:

Distant Past | **Recent Past** | **Present** | **Near Future** | **Distant Future**

The issue as other people see it:

Distant Past | **Recent Past** | **Present** | **Near Future** | **Distant Future**

Card Reversals

The difference between an upright and reversed Tarot card is obvious: When you look at the card its picture is either right side up or upside down. Whether a card turns upright or reversed depends on whether you turn around the cards when you shuffle a pack. Many Tarot books tell you that when a card lands right side up this is positive, and when it is reversed this is negative. For example, the Two of Pentacles carries the idea of enjoying life and keeping everything in balance. Reversed, it means that the balance is lost and happiness is lost. Sometimes, though, if a card has a negative meaning, reversing it can suggest signs of improvement. For example, if you turn the Ten of Swords upside down you can see that the swords fall out of the man's back. Why not look through the pack yourself and see what happens to the pictures when you turn them upside down? Is the situation improved, or is it made worse?

We don't really recommend card reversals because every card has both a negative and a positive aspect. It's the same in life. You can always find the positive in the negative and the negative in the positive. For example, suppose Simon's parents divorce and he goes to live with his mom. This isn't good news for Simon, but the upside is no more arguments and tension. Suppose Rebecca gets a lucrative modeling contract. This is great, but the downside is not being able to finish her exams at school and being apart from her family for long periods of time.

We all want to have fun in life. No one likes to suffer. But as we stressed in the last section, sometimes pain is necessary to help us move on. For example, Tamzin is going out with a great-looking guy named Paul. Trouble is, Paul won't let her have her own point of view. Tamzin needs to go through the pain of confronting him, and if after that he just carries on in his old ways, she needs to leave him. It would be very bad for her self-esteem to carry on with the situation as it is. She needs to face a little pain in her life in order to learn and grow as a person. If you are doing readings for yourself, try to be very honest and admit that sometimes it is necessary to experience things you don't like for your life to move forward. It's the same if you are doing readings for someone else. Gently remind that person that setbacks are often inevitable, but there is always an upside if they decide to look for it.

If you still want to use reversed cards in your readings, make sure you shuffle the cards thoroughly, turning them as well. Then when you lay the cards down, turn them from side to side, as if you are reading a book, so that you don't change the way the card was laid down.

Quick Fun Reading

Shuffle your pack and chose three cards at random. Reverse them and think of as many negative meanings as you can for each card. Now think about incidents in your past that these cards could reflect. What good came out of these situations for you? However grim things appear, there is always something good. Often, though, you can see this only in retrospect. Aren't you glad now that you moved on from your first boyfriend or girlfriend? Remember how devastated you were at the time? Think about those exams you failed years ago. Didn't they help you work harder? Remind yourself in times of sadness and uncertainty that although you don't know it now, good things can and do lie ahead. It's just that you can't see the bigger picture right now.

17
Reading the Cards

Reading the cards is not about memorizing each card's meaning. One picture can be interpreted in so many ways that this just isn't possible. When you start doing readings, don't get overwhelmed and panicky because you don't understand what a card is trying to say. Working with the Tarot is just like getting to know a new friend. It takes time.

People often ask us why Tarot readings work. The answer is simple. They work because you want them to. Approaching the cards with the intention of discovering something about yourself and your life is the key. If you still have any doubt or a "show me" attitude, you really are wasting your time.

It's best to start with a really simple three-card spread, like the one mentioned in the previous chapter. You may even want to just pick one card and spend time thinking about that. As you feel more comfortable, increase the number of cards you use. You may also want to work with just one part of the deck first, say the Major, Minor, or Court cards. Doing this will help you get to know the deck.

Remember that it is good to have a question in mind when you approach the cards and to remember that every situation has a positive message and a negative one. Think of the cards as a magic mirror that can give you a new perspective on yourself and your life. When you start working with spreads, you should use the following guidelines:

- Start by interpreting the first thoughts and feelings that come to the surface.
- Look at the interpretations in this book to see if any concepts or questions seem relevant to you.
- Keep a record of your interpretations so you can refer back to them.

If you don't like what you are reading, think about how to make things different. Often this means changing your attitude toward something or someone. If you just don't know what the cards are saying, slow down. Leave the card in question out where you can see it, and come back to it later. It might also help to get someone else to give their thoughts about the card. It's amazing how another person's thoughts and ideas can spark your own. If after all this you still aren't sure, ask the cards to give you clarity, and select one more card whose meaning may provide that clarity.

Sample Spreads

Here are two sample spreads using the Celtic Cross and the specific-issues spread (both are shown in Chapter 16). We hope they will get you thinking along the right lines and give you an idea of how the bigger Tarot spreads can work. For these and any other spreads you choose, get in the habit of turning the cards from side to side, instead of flipping them over; turn them as you would turn the pages of a book. This avoids the problem of card reversals, which we also discussed in Chapter 16. And when you put your cards away afterward, don't forget to thank them and to close your reading in a spirit of gratitude.

The Celtic Cross

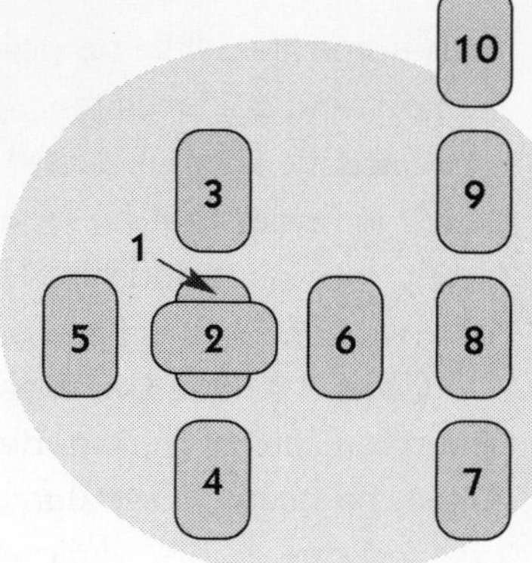

Let's say this reading is for Mark, seventeen years old, who is thinking about leaving home and moving in with his girlfriend.

Card 1: General situation. Mark chose The Magician. The Magician makes things happen. Mark has set his mind on moving out, and this is clearly what he wants to do.

Card 2: Obstacles that lie in Mark's path. The Knight of Swords indicates that Mark is somebody who is always in a hurry. He doesn't always think about the consequences of his actions. Is moving in with his girlfriend really the right thing for him to do? Has he thought things through?

Card 3: The past. Mark's card here is The Star, suggesting that his relationship with his girlfriend began with great hope for the future.

Card 4: Influences working in Mark's favor. Mark chose the Ten of Cups. This is the card of home and family, suggesting that whatever decision he makes, he will have the support and love of his family behind him.

Card 5: Near future. The Ten of Swords suggests that Mark has started to get anxious about the situation. Is it really practical to move in with his girlfriend when he still has to work his way through college?

Card 6: The distant future. Mark chose the King of Wands. This suggests that Mark will feel energized by the decision he eventually makes, but he needs to make sure that his newfound power doesn't go to his head.

Card 7: Himself. Mark chose the Eight of Wands, which shows that he is the kind of person who easily rushes into things.

Card 8: His home. The Ten of Pentacles suggests that Mark finds home life a little restrictive. He doesn't fully appreciate the love, support, and guidance that are there for him if only he would ask.

Card 9: His hopes and fears. Mark chose the Queen of Cups, which indicates that he longs for his independence and to be in a happy, loving relationship. The danger is that he is letting his feelings take over, and is living in a dream world.

Card 10: The eventual outcome. Mark chose The Moon. The Moon is a card of illusion. Before Mark makes any decision about his future, he needs to see things as they really are and ask himself lots of questions. Is his relationship with his girlfriend sound? Has he thought through the practicalities? Apart from this relationship, what does he want to do with the rest of his life? Why is he so eager to leave home before his studies are complete? Has he really thought things through?

The Specific-Issues Spread

June, fifteen, has been having problems with her boyfriend. She wants the cards to tell her if their relationship has a future. The cards that show how the issue looks from her perspective are The Emperor (Distant Past), Six of Wands (Recent Past), Five of Swords (Present), Nine of Wands (Near Future), and Queen of Swords (Distant Future). The Emperor suggests that in all matters to do with men she is very influenced by her father. He is a very severe man and she expects all men to behave like him. The Six of Wands reflects the joy that both June and her boyfriend felt when they met. The Five of Swords indicates all the current troubles. Notice that June feels that her boyfriend is walking away from her after having stolen her heart. The Nine of Wands indicates that the relationship could survive, but both need to work at it. The Queen of Swords is not a happy ending. It seems to suggest that if the effort is not made, there could be a painful breakup.

The cards indicating the relationship from the boyfriend's point of view are the Four of Wands (Distant Past), Three of Cups (Recent

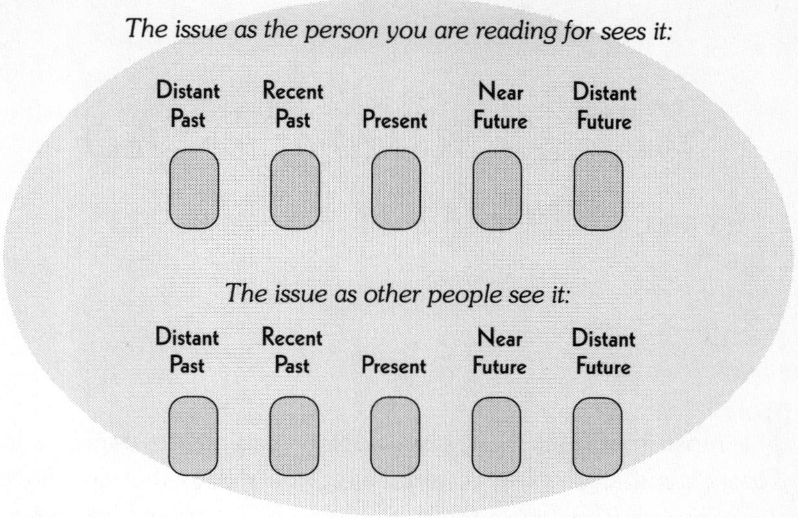

The issue as the person you are reading for sees it:

Distant Past | Recent Past | Present | Near Future | Distant Future

The issue as other people see it:

Distant Past | Recent Past | Present | Near Future | Distant Future

Past), Three of Swords (Present), Eight of Swords (Near Future), and The Empress (Distant Future). The Four of Wands indicates that the boyfriend looks at a past before he met his girlfriend as an uncomplicated, happy time. The Three of Cups indicates the very real passion he felt for her when he meet her. The present (Three of Swords) shows that the relationship is really hurting him, and the Eight of Swords suggests that if something isn't done, things will get worse. By contrast, The Empress indicates that in the distant future he will be happy again. Whether or not it is with June depends on how willing they are to work together on the relationship.

18 How to Do Readings for Your Friends and Family

The most important thing about doing readings for family and friends is that you feel comfortable. That means that you have someplace comfortable and quiet to sit and you don't feel forced into it. Tarot card reading can be exhausting. If you don't feel in the mood, don't do it just to please others.

Only read for friends and family who are really interested and who take the whole thing seriously. If they are receptive, explain to them that you have just started, so they need to bear with you a little. Explain that a Tarot reading is a two-way process and that they should ask lots of questions. You might well find that as you are going on they also start interpreting the meanings of the cards themselves. Encourage this, because their understanding of the meanings of the cards will help you.

Ask them to shuffle the cards and think about the question they want to ask. Then you can either get them to choose the cards, or you can pick the first card from the top of the deck—whatever works best for you. Then, as you do your reading, keep these cautionary tips in mind:

- If you do a reading for someone else you take on a big responsibility. Don't abuse it. Never present information as the absolute truth or suggest there is no room for choice. The cards only give one way of looking at problems. They don't have all the answers.

- You are not a doctor, lawyer, accountant, or teacher. If the person you are reading for wants guidance about health, legal, financial, or academic issues, encourage them to talk to the specialist concerned.
- If someone is in danger, get help. If you believe that someone is in danger of harming himself or herself or another person, report the situation to that person's family or the proper authorities as soon as possible.
- Don't get out of your depth. If you aren't comfortable discussing certain areas of a person's life, tell them.
- Be diplomatic. Be motivated by love and compassion. You don't want to alarm or panic anyone. Sometimes you have to say something that the person you're reading for may not want to hear. Be very careful with the way you word things. Never say, "This will definitely happen." Say something more gentle, like "The card suggests you could be heading for burnout. What do you think about that?"

There will be times when you will stumble and find yourself reaching for words. Don't be frightened about saying the first thing that comes to mind. The Tarot works best when you rely on your first impressions. If you are worried about what to say next or, even worse, rehearse what you are going to say, it is not working. The Tarot is very much about going with the flow. Nothing should feel forced or difficult. Most of us are lucky enough to be able to walk without thinking about it. That's what you have to aim for with the Tarot. You need to become so familiar with your Tarot deck and so inspired by the pictures on the cards that you can talk about them without effort.

Above all, remember to be positive and upbeat. This advice

applies to readings you do for yourself as well. Every card has a range of negative and positive possibilities, and you, as a reader, have a duty to stress the positive. You can mention the negative, but let them know that we all can make positive choices. We find that the word *but* can be very useful. For example, if the person you are reading for draws the Three of Swords, don't say, "You feel really hurt and upset and will feel like this for quite a while." Say something like, "There will be pain and heartache, *but* you will be able to learn from the experience and find something better to replace what you have lost." And, finally, if the person you are reading for wants you to help with an important decision—for example, Should I leave him or stay?—your task is not to tell her what to do, but to help her explore the pros and cons of each choice and then search within her heart for the best possible solution.

The Really Big Fun Exercise

Now is the time to take the plunge and do your first reading. If you have gotten this far in the book, then you know more than most people do about the Tarot. Start practicing on yourself and then ask a few friends if you can practice on them. Try using the three-card layout and see what happens. You never know—you may surprise yourself and your friends!

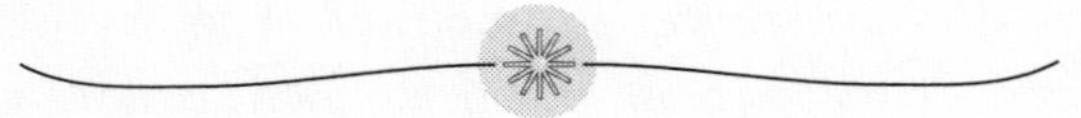

Part Four

Making the Tarot Work for You

✷ Tarot readings have been described as laying out your dreams and for me the Tarot is primarily a personal guide.

—Cassandra Eason, *Complete Book of Tarot*

19 Personal Life

Dating, Love, and Sex

We've started this section with dating, love, and sex because, let's face it, it's on your mind most of the time. And if you start to read cards for other people, you will almost certainly find that many of the questions you are asked are about love—how to find it and how to keep it. Will I ever have a boyfriend or girlfriend? Does he or she like me? Is this going to last forever?

Quick Fun Exercise: Who Is Your Ideal Date?

Remove all the Major Arcana, and shuffle the Minor Arcana. Now choose one card:

If you get a Sword, you like dark types.
If you get a Cup, you go for blond types.
If you get a Pentacle, you like them well built.
If you get a Wand, you like them slim.

Pick a second card:

If you get a Sword, you like the intellectual types.
If you get a Cup, you go for emotional types.
If you get a Pentacle, you like practical types.
If you get a Wand, you like energetic types.

Obviously there are certain cards in the pack, like The Lovers and the suit of Cups, that focus more on love and close relationships than others, but don't be surprised if you ask the cards a question about relationships and just a few or none of these cards appear. This doesn't mean you are going to end up alone. What the cards may be suggesting is that now isn't the best time for love, and it might be good to put your energies into other things. It isn't wise for you to center your life around love, sex, and dating.

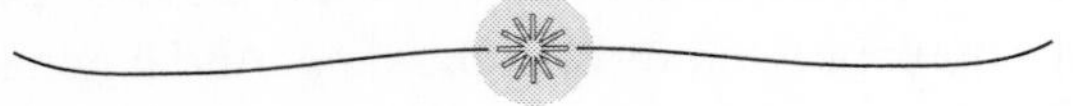

The more you center your life on someone or the more you hope for someone ideal to appear, the more unattractive or unappealing you become to the very people you want to attract. Not sure what we mean? Well, if love, sex, and dating are all you think about, you just end up looking desperate. It's also quite irritating when someone builds his or her life around you. When you become the center of someone else's life they are getting all their security from you, not from themselves. Then every so often there is one of those horrible "where do I stand" talks.

If you are in a relationship and you are constantly breaking up and getting back together, the chances are that either you or your partner or both of you are too centered on each other. The two of you have gotten so wrapped up in each other that neither of you can let go. If you aren't in a relationship and feel wretched because you haven't got a date, the chances are you are centering your life too much on the idea of a relationship. Any reading you do will almost certainly reflect this imbalance back to you.

Believe us, you'll be a better boyfriend or girlfriend if you are not centered on your partner. You will also be far more attractive to a potential partner if you look like you have a life and aren't waiting for someone else to make you live it. Independence is far more attractive than dependence. Dependence isn't really love; it is a bit like an addiction.

This doesn't mean you shouldn't date or ask the cards about your close relationships. Of course you should. It just means that you should not get obsessed with or center your life around someone else. The same applies to sex. Whether you are in a relationship or not, the issue of sex is always there. Should you or shouldn't you? Nobody can make that decision for you, but try to remember that having sex will not make you feel like an adult. It will not make someone love you. It will not change your life. Sex is also about more than your body. It is about your heart, whether you are a boy or a girl. What you decide to do about sex will affect your self-image and your relationships with others more than any other decision you make. So if you do ask the cards about sex, you can be sure that they will always urge you to search your heart and think about it—very carefully.

The Relationship Spread

The specific-issues spread is often used to discuss relationships. The cards are laid into two rows of five cards. The upper row represents how you feel about relationships, or, if you are reading for someone else, how they feel about relationships. The lower row represents the relationship from the point of view of the other person involved. This person may be someone you already know. If you aren't in a relationship it could represent someone you are hoping to meet, or it could suggest ways to improve your chances of having a relationship.

Card 1 in each row represents the origins of the relationship.
Card 2 represents where it is coming from.
Card 3 represents the way things are now.
Card 4 indicates where the relationship is going.
Card 5 indicates how it ultimately evolves.

You will find that this reading gives you lots to think about. Have fun! It might help to write down what you think the cards are trying to tell you and discuss them with your partner, if you have one, or a close friend.

Parents, Home, and Adults

The Tarot cards, particularly the Swords, do show images of conflict and aggression. Conflict occurs when people feel misunderstood. No one starts a war or an argument for fun. People have to have some grievance, which makes them behave in an aggressive way. In short, violence and conflict often result from misunderstandings.

The teenage years tend to be the time of maximum conflict with parents, authority figures, or adults in general. They want one thing, and you want something else. They want you to do what they think is right, and you want to do what you think is right. Neither party seems to understand the other. So how do we get to the Ten of Cups or the Ten of Pentacles, where we see adults and young people interacting happily? How can the cards help you?

First of all, working with the cards will help you start to see that there are many ways to look at a situation. Why not look at things from your parents' point of view for a change? If you think it is hard being a teenager, try being an adult—all those commitments and pressures and responsibilities. Why not try listening to what they have to say? This doesn't mean agreeing. It means just listening and understanding and respecting that they have pressures just like you. When you respect and understand someone it is much easier to talk to them. It also encourages them to respect and understand you. Remember that you teach other people how to treat you by the way you behave.

The way you respond to your parents influences the reaction you get from them. For example, suppose you want to talk to your mom and she half ignores you because she is busy paying the bills. If you leave the room, you have taught her that if she ignores you, you will go away. If you yell and scream at your parents, you have taught them that you are childlike and irresponsible. If you are willing to listen to other people's point of views, stand up for yourself, and demonstrate that you are mature and responsible, you'll soon find that adults will start to take you seriously.

Time and time again in a reading the cards will suggest to you that you are responsible for the way your parents or other adults treat you. You are teaching them or allowing them to react to you in a certain way. If you don't like the way your parents are treating you, if you don't like the situation at home, if you hate your brothers and sisters, the answer isn't to rebel, come home late, or run away to get them to see your point of view. The answer is to change the way you behave. And the Tarot is great at suggesting ways you can do this.

Important note. We are of course talking about a home environment that is fair-minded and caring. If you feel trapped or in danger and can't get anyone to listen to you, put your Tarot cards down and confide in an adult you trust. Take care of yourself. You are worth it. Here are some numbers that might help:

Rape, abuse, and incest
1-800-656-4673

Neglect
1-800-422-4453

Violence
1-800-799-7233

Suicide
1-888-793-4357

Quick Fun Exercise

Choose two or three Court cards to represent yourself and the significant adults in your family life. Don't choose them by shuffling, but look through the Court cards to choose cards that best represent them and you. David chooses King of Pentacles for his dad because his dad is practical and down to earth. He chooses Knight of Cups for himself because he sees himself as a bit of a dreamer.

Now you need to shuffle the cards and think about what you need to do to improve the relationship. David got the Ace of Pentacles. The Pentacles suggest a practical, down-to-earth approach, and the Ace is one of the strongest of the Pentacles. In this case, if David is to have better conversations and experiences with his dad, he needs to approach him in a straightforward, practical, and down-to-earth way. Basically, he needs to say what he means and ask for help and support if he needs it. His dad isn't a mind reader.

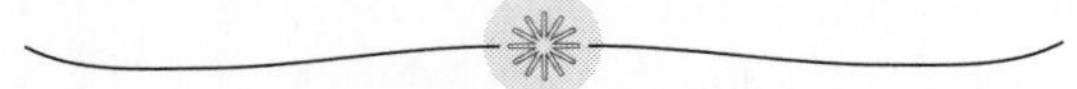

Friends

Friends are important—never more so than when you are a teenager. There is nothing better than feeling like you belong and are accepted. There is nothing worse than feeling like a loner.

What Kind of Friend?

If you want to ask the cards a question about a friend, the Celtic Cross spread might be a good choice. For position one, choose a Court card that best represents the friend you want to think about, and then choose the remaining nine cards from the rest of the pack. The following might help you choose:

- Pages indicate someone quite young and impressionable.
- Knights indicate someone who prefers to lead rather than follow.
- Queens represent someone who is sociable.

- Kings represent someone who is capable and responsible.
  - Page of Wands: A friendly individual, always laughing and a bit of a joker.
  - Page of Swords: Enjoys an argument, and can be quite cutting at times.
  - Page of Cups: A dreamy individual who finds it difficult to settle.
  - Page of Pentacles: Intelligent, but lacks common sense.
  - Knight of Wands: Loves adventure and fun.
  - Knight of Swords: Quick to make decisions; a fast runner.
  - Knight of Cups: Can be imaginative; perhaps drinks too much.
  - Knight of Pentacles: Very set in his ways.
  - Queen of Wands: An extrovert.
  - Queen of Swords: A cynic.
  - Queen of Cups: A very sensitive person.
  - Queen of Pentacles: Healthy, outdoors type.
  - King of Wands: Optimistic and energetic.
  - King of Swords: Critical but fair.
  - King of Cups: Kind and generous. Often ends up helping others.
  - King of Pentacles: Very practical, and pays attention to detail.

What Kind of Friend Are You?

Take only the Court cards out of the pack. Shuffle them all, and place one on the left, one on the right. The one on the left represents the kind of friend you are. The one on the right represent the friends you want to attract into your life.

Remember, when you choose a card to represent a friend or yourself, it isn't fixed in stone. People can and do change. You aren't stuck with that card, and can choose another one later. Part of being a teenager is trying on different personalities. A lot depends on the group of people you hang out with, or whom you may be interacting with. At home you might have an older brother or sister, which means you hardly get a word in edgewise. That all changes when you are at school. Most of your classmates are very quiet, which makes you the talkative one. You may also react to teachers differently. Some inspire confidence in you; others inspire fear. The great thing about being a teenager is that you can reinvent yourself.

Important note: Bullying is the exception to the law of reciprocity. Nobody deserves to be treated badly and unfairly. If you, or someone you know, is being treated unjustly and unfairly, put the cards down and immediately seek help and advice from an adult you can trust.

When you do readings, you will notice time and time again that the cards urge you to have a balanced approach to life. Friends are great, but if you base your identity on the group you hang out with, you may find yourself doing things you don't want to do. Make friends, but don't make them the center of your world. Why? Because—believe it or not—some years from now you may not even remember their names. A few friendships from school days survive, but the great majority don't. People move on, and so should you.

If you are having problems with your friends, the cards will urge you to take the lead—to stop complaining or worrying about your friendships and to start controlling them. It is up to you to renegotiate with your friends to get the treatment you want and deserve. Always remember that the most important relationship you have is the one you have with yourself, and it is the one that sets the tone for all the other relationships in your life. Everyone in your life will see how you treat yourself, what you expect of yourself, and whether you can stand up for yourself. If you treat yourself with respect, you signal to others that you are a person who is to be treated with respect.

Working with the Tarot is all about helping you understand who you are and what you want from your life. The more firm you are in your convictions, the less willing you will be to let people into your life who will pressure you or try to manipulate you. Let the cards teach you the principle of reciprocity: In life you always get what you give. How can other people give you what you won't give yourself?

Health and Appearance

The Tarot is all about sorting out the inner person and being positive and hopeful about your life. It's a cliché and you have probably heard it time and time and time again, but it's true: It's what's inside that counts. If you feel lousy on the inside, however hard you try, you won't look good on the outside. The important thing is feeling good physically, not looking good to others. So before you start comparing yourself to your friends, please remember that you don't have to look a certain way to be happy.

This isn't to say that looking good isn't important. We all know that it is. Just remember that if you don't feel good on the inside, it doesn't matter what you look like on the outside. A major part of feeling good on the inside is learning how to take care of yourself. Once again the Tarot will remind you of the principle of balance. You need to learn to relax and take time to treat yourself to some tender loving care. How? Use your common sense: eat healthful food; get enough sleep; exercise regularly; say no to drugs, smoking, and alcohol; use your brain; surround yourself with those who care about you; and find some interest or hobby that inspires you. Basically, lead a balanced, healthy life.

The Tarot will always advise you to take responsibility for your health. Sometimes it may highlight particular health issues and concerns. Remember, though, that you are not a doctor, and the cards are not a source of medical information. If there is anything worrying you, see a doctor as soon as possible.

If the following cards appear in a reading, take note. They *may* indicate the following:

- The Empress: You might be drawn toward natural medicine.
- The Lovers: Take care with sexually transmitted diseases.

- Strength: Sore throats.
- The Hermit: Weight problems or eating disorders—make sure you talk to your doctor if this is the case.
- The Devil: Stay away from drugs and alcohol.
- The Moon: Stay away from drugs and alcohol.
- Two of Swords: Eye problems.
- Two of Pentacles: Colds/flu.
- Three of Swords: Take care of your heart; make sure you get lots of exercise, and stay away from fatty foods.
- Four of Pentacles: Possible stomach upsets.
- Four of Swords: A visit to the dentist might be wise.
- Five of Wands: Headaches/acne.
- Five of Cups: You could be feeling a bit low emotionally. Talk to an adult you trust.
- Five of Pentacles: Aches and pains in the lower part of your body.
- Six of Pentacles: Knee problems.
- Eight of Swords: Back problems.
- Eight of Pentacles: Be careful with your hands.
- Nine of Wands: Headaches/acne.
- Nine of Swords: Headaches/acne and severe backache.
- Ten of Swords: PMS.
- King of Pentacles: Hearing problems.

Fun Exercise

Pick out some of the cards listed above, and look carefully at the shapes, colors, and pictures. See if you can understand why those particular cards could suggest the health issues mentioned. Then look through the pack yourself, and see if you can link certain health matters to certain cards. Write down your thoughts. They may come in handy when you do a reading.

20 School and Career

School

If you consult the cards about issues related to school, work, or exams, bear in mind that the Tarot is first and foremost about the universality of life, and not really about what goes on at school. Yes, school is extremely important, but there is also a great big world out there where you will one day make your mark, and the Tarot will tend to focus on that.

Your education is vital to your future and should be a priority, but don't get so hung up on grades, impressing teachers, and passing exams that you forget that the whole point of school is to learn. This is where the cards can help you, or the person you're reading for. Every reading having to do with school, teachers, or exams will remind you that you can do very well in school and still have a healthy balance in life.

If you do want to ask the cards about schoolwork, teachers, or exams, it might be best to first choose a card that represents schoolwork or a particular teacher to you. For example, all of the Pages and all of the cards in the suit of Pentacles might indicate learning and studying. A principal might be represented by The Emperor; an artistic, nature-loving teacher might be represented by the Queen of Pentacles. Once you have chosen a card, put it in position one for the Celtic Cross reading, and choose nine other cards to finish the spread.

As stressed earlier, if you are doing a reading for someone else, remember to always be positive. We are not advising you to lie. If you see that someone is having difficulty with a question about an assignment, say so, but remember that your words will have great impact. Sometimes failing an assignment can be a wonderful learning experience. You can find out what you need to do to succeed next time. Also, students should never be afraid to try new things and fail. You will never find a safer environment than school, where you can fail with so few consequences. Out in the real world failing often costs a whole load of money, stress, and disappointment. Encourage the people you read for to enjoy what they are doing at school and to try as many things as they can, even if they are afraid of failing. Never again will you have the time to experience so many different subjects at no cost.

Many school questions involve issues of personalities. Bullying is often the reality of life in school. It is important to realize that the Tarot by itself will not keep unpleasant incidents from happening at school. It might, however, alert you to problems. You or the person you are reading for should always talk to adults if you are in any kind of distress. Many of the cards do suggest seeking out a wise person to advise you. These cards are a direct response to the problems being discussed and should not be ignored. Tarot is not about being stuck with problems and not resolving them. It is very solution-focused, and your seeking help from an adult is often part of the solution.

Quick Fun Exercise

Shuffle the cards of the Major Arcana and pick one. The card chosen represents the subject you will excel in next semester. If you don't study that subject, think of a subject that you do study that is similar.

- The Fool: Art
- The Magician: Drama
- The High Priestess: History
- The Empress: Home economics
- The Emperor: Math
- The Hierophant: Religious education
- The Lovers: Biology
- The Chariot: Geography
- Strength: Physical education
- The Hermit: English literature
- Wheel of Fortune: Foreign languages
- Justice: Debating
- The Hanged Man: Physics
- Death: Chemistry
- Temperance: English
- The Devil: Business studies
- The Tower: Debating
- The Star: Philosophy
- The Moon: Design
- The Sun: Information technology
- Judgement: School or community activities
- The World: Every subject

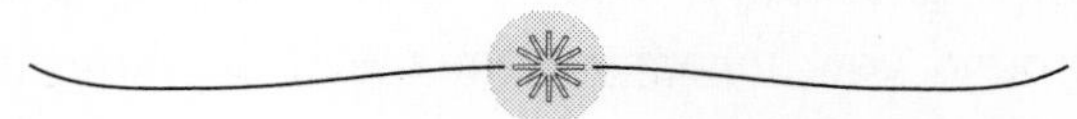

Money

The Pentacles are the Minor Arcana cards associated with money. Whenever they appear in a reading, these cards are telling you to pay attention to your finances in some way. Chances are, the message will be strong and clear: Enjoy money and the choices it makes available to you, but don't center your life on material things.

We live in a world that teaches us that the fastest car, the nicest clothes, the best haircut, the latest computer, and the many other things that money can buy will bring happiness. The sad thing is, they don't. Possessions can also come to you in the form of titles, such as class president, cheerleader, student officer, and so on. It's fine to enjoy money, and there is nothing wrong with accomplishing things, but the Tarot is wise when it warns us not to let our lives revolve around things that aren't of lasting value. Good feelings about yourself have to come from within, not from the things that you have.

> When I got my car I was thrilled. My friend Mark was so jealous. He wasn't allowed to have one until he was eighteen. All year he was aggressive toward me. It got to the point where I wished I didn't have the car if it meant we could have our friendship back. When he finally got his car it was all he talked about. Then he had an accident and died. Shame that all I could remember about him were the events of the past year. I'd forgotten what a nice person he used to be before he got so fixated on cars.—Simon, seventeen

If you identify yourself by what you have and what you do, what happens when you lose that? Who are you? Don't be like Mark in the story above, and want something so badly that it makes you and everyone around you unhappy. Remember, the best things in life, such as friendship and love, can never be bought.

Fun Exercise

Find the Ace, Four, Five, and Six of Pentacles. Then read the four statements below and see if you can match one of these cards to each of the statements. Really look at the cards. Be aware of the shape, movement, and colors of your cards.

- We are going to get rich, whatever the cost.
- Money is not important. We want to have fun and enjoy our life.
- We are just going to try to get by and hope that family or the state can help us out.
- We work hard, save money when we can, but we also make sure we enjoy ourselves.

Which of the above statements do you, or your family, live by?

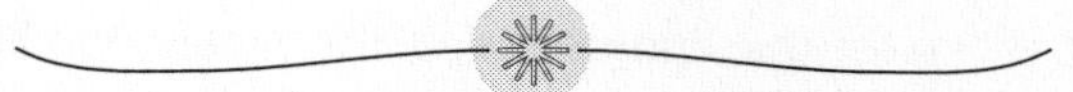

The relationship you have with money is an important one. You can get obsessed with it, save it, and never spend it. The trouble with this is that we miss out on the important things in life. Think about a dad who misses out on seeing his kids because he is always working. Look at the Four of Pentacles. This guy is holding life so tightly and in such a possessive way that he is not enjoying it. Remember that the greatest gift we have is time. A part-time job is good, but don't spend all your hours working at a fast-food joint. Schedule some time for fun as well. We work to live; we don't live to work.

On the other hand, you could go the other way and place too little value on money. Yes, the best things in life are free. The air that we breathe is free. Nature is free. Love is free. However, if you and your family want to go to a park, you need to have clothes and shoes to wear, gas for the car if you are driving there, and gear if you want to go camping. You can't get away from it: You need money to survive. Many relationships break down through the hardship of poverty. So if you are one of those people who don't save at all and just spend, spend, spend, or max out credit cards with massive interest rates, you will end up like the guys in the Five of Pentacles—the card of financial hardship. This is where you could end up if you spend all your money, don't bother about schoolwork, and live only in the here and now. Take a good long look at the card. It is not a good place to be.

Your attitude toward money also could be rather childlike: "Somebody please take care of me." If it isn't family, it can be welfare. Yes, our families are there to support us, but we can never fully grow into independent adults as long as we keep coming back to Mommy or Daddy for a cash fix. Relying on welfare is just as bad. Welfare should be relied on only as a temporary relief or in cases of real need or disability. The Six of Pentacles shows people receiving money. Just look at the figures doing the receiving. They looked hunched and desperate. Note that they are on the ground kneeling. This suggests how inferior and childlike they feel. Growing up is all about taking responsibility for yourself. Though complete financial independence is many years ahead of you, you must see it as a goal you are aiming for.

Finally, we come to the Ace of Pentacles. It can be surprising to see the tremendous rewards that careful management of money can yield over the years. Many times it is just a matter of thinking before you spend, and getting your priorities right. Often this can be done by cutting back on a few luxuries. Do you need to buy that cup of coffee on the way to school? Do you really need to smoke? It's amazing how quickly small savings mount up. Over a couple of months they might add up to hundreds of dollars. Maybe you could use the money saved to buy a present for your mom and dad to say thank you for everything they have done for you, or you could use it to buy yourself a fabulous new outfit. The important thing is that you are learning to respect and value money. The Ace of Pentacles is an optimistic and golden card. It shows that keeping a careful eye on money while at the same time enjoying life is ideal.

Work

The suit of the Minor Arcana associated with work or career is the suit of Wands. Whenever they appear in a reading, the chances are the cards are telling you to pay attention to the work you do. The message will be strong and clear: work to live, don't live to work.

Actual paid work is probably a small part of your life at the moment, or you may be just launching yourself into a job or career. It is good to have a small part-time job to give you a little bit of money. However, if it is taking up too much time, eating into your school life, home life, and fun life, then it is getting out of balance. You don't want to get into that rat race too early. And when you do eventually settle into your career, you want to make sure that you keep that work-to-life balance going. Becoming work-centered is a sickness that affects lots of adults, but it can also hit teens. Workaholism is usually driven by a need to have more things, like money, cars, status, or recognition. The trouble with these things is that they can't really satisfy you.

You may think that a career can provide you with the stability you need in life. In some respects it does. You can pay your way and take charge of your life in a way you were not able to before, and you get recognition for doing it. That's why it is important to have career aspirations and goals, and to strive for success. Just remember, though, that there is a fine line between trying to obtain something and letting your whole world revolve around it. The latter is something you should not do. It's like worshipping a movie star or rock star who one day does something stupid and dies or ends up in jail. Where does that leave you? It is dangerous to let your life revolve around anything but your own values and principles.

What are principles? They are things like honesty, love, discipline, loyalty, and integrity. There are lots of others, and your heart will easily recognize them. To grasp why a life that isn't based on them won't work, think of a life based on their opposites: dishonesty, hatred indulgence, ingratitude, and so on. In this book you may have already noticed that all of the cards are based upon one or more principles. That is where their power and magic come from.

Fun Exercise

Find the Six, Seven, Nine, and Ten of Wands, and then match them up with the four statements below.

"I enjoy my work. I work part-time in a shoe shop at the mall. It has taught me how a small business is run." Sarah, sixteen

"My job is hard. I wash cars downtown for my uncle. I work on the highway; sometimes I don't feel safe." Tom, seventeen

"I help out at my local theater. The hours are long but I am going to be a performer. It is my life." Marie, thirteen

"I can't cope. I'm working too many hours." Lucy, fifteen

If you enjoy something, you tend to be quite good at it. Sarah sees her job as a learning experience. Her employers, parents, and customers have noted her enthusiastic approach. This kind of attitude will take her far. The Six of Wands is the card for success.

Tom, on the other hand, is doing a job that is dangerous. He should stop it at once. Self-esteem is an important issue in jobs. It is important that you don't feel forced into jobs because of pressure from others. It is also important that you don't just accept the first thing that comes along just to get some money. The Seven of Wands suggests a dangerous situation that needs to be dealt with immediately.

Marie sounds fine until the last sentence, where we hear her say that performing is her life. Many people get their identity from what they do. When you are a little older you will find that people go to parties and introduce themselves by profession: "I am a doctor." "I am a salesperson." The trouble with this is that nothing in life is permanent. Most things get taken away from us at some time. Even if you do the same job until you retire, there comes a time when you will have to ask yourself, Who am I when the job is taken away from me? The Nine of Wands shows somebody who is competent at what they do, but unhappy. They hold onto their stick very fiercely because it is all they know. They are ready to use it to fight off anybody who comes close to them. This could mean using work as a way of keeping people from finding out who you really are.

Lucy needs to learn to say no, just as Tom does. If you do too much, everything suffers. It is important to set a list of priorities and put first things first. Schoolwork should be number one on your to-do list. It is pointless to earn only a few dollars when a high school diploma could open the doors to better-paid work in the future. You will notice that the person in the Ten of Wands is carrying a heavy load. If he keeps on carrying these ten wands, chances are he is going to fall over because it is all too heavy for him. The Ten of Wands teaches an important lesson. Work should be a fun, enjoyable part of life (although every job has its dull moments), but it should never be allowed to take over your life. Later, when you leave school and start to make your contribution to the world, finding the right balance between work and your life outside of work will be crucial for your health, happiness, and success.

21 Emotions

Worries and Fears

We all have worries and fears. Some of us are just better than others at focusing on the positive.

Quick Fun Exercise

Shuffle the pack and concentrate on everything that is worrying you. Pick a card. Shuffle again but this time think about what your hopes and dreams are. Pick another card. Then shuffle again and think about what you want to do with your life. Pick a third card. Now use the earlier chapters in this book to work out what the cards are saying. Take your time and really think about the card and what you think it might be trying to tell you.

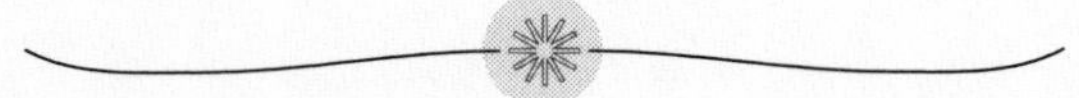

Rhina picked the Ten of Cups for her worries, Temperance for her hopes, and the Ten of Swords for what she is going to do with her life.

Temperance is telling her that she hopes to be thought of as a kind and caring person. She may even be attracted to the caring professions later in life, like nursing or counseling. She has a patient nature and will do very well in it. The Ten of Cups, as her worry card, is the card of a happy home, which Rhina has. We reversed the meaning of this card (there is more about that in Chapter 16) because the question was about worries, and a happy family can't be a problem. Then the card suggested that she should seek out role models outside her family who can help her take the first steps toward independence. The Ten of Swords seems to say on the surface that her life will be one disaster after another. However, if you turn the picture around all the swords fall out. Rhina has a number of obstacles ahead, but the future is bright if she seeks support and works hard to achieve her dreams.

So how do you conquer your worries and look on the bright side? The Aces in the Tarot pack offer some advice here. Search through your pack, and look at the Ace of Wands, Pentacles, Swords, and Cups. You will notice that they are all clear, bright, strong, and filled with purpose. If something is bothering you, it might help to take a good long look at one of these cards to see if it can give you a sense of purpose. Worry has no purpose. It doesn't achieve anything, and it doesn't help anyone, especially not you. So the next time worry strikes, stop. Find out what is worrying you. If you can do something, think through the pros and cons and make a decision. If it is the wrong decision, use the setback as a learning experience and try again to find a solution. If, however, you can't do anything about what is worrying you, let the worry go.

Quick Fun Exercise

Pick the Ten of Swords, Nine of Swords, and The Devil. Look at them quickly—you don't want to dwell too long on cards with negative energy—and think about what these cards remind you of in your life. Perhaps it's a poor exam result, a nasty hangover, or an argument with your mom. When you think about these unhappy incidents, how could you have handled things better? What did you learn from them? Why was it important for you to experience these unhappy things?

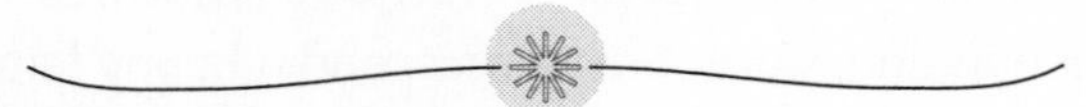

When James, fourteen, looked at these cards, they reminded him of waiting for exam results (Nine of Swords), being assaulted by some older kids in the mall (Ten of Swords), and doing very badly in high school baseball tryouts (The Devil). He realized with the Nine of Swords that worrying about the exam was futile—not just because he had already taken the exam and there was nothing he could do about it, but because he actually did very well. The Ten of Swords told him there was not much he could do about the episode at the mall; he was just unlucky and in the wrong place at the wrong time. He did learn from the experience, though, and is quick to intervene if he sees someone being picked on at school. The Devil upset James. He is still upset about not making the baseball team, and hasn't wanted to play baseball since. What he could learn from this is that if he really wants something, he should keep trying. Both the Beatles and J. K. Rowling, the creator of Harry Potter, were rejected by practically every company around before they landed their first contracts. They went on to become millionaires several times over, leaving those who rejected them feeling rather foolish. Elvis Presley was told by his music teacher that he couldn't sing. We all know that he became a legend. James should remind himself that the road to success is often paved with failure, but you are never really a failure until you stop trying.

Remember that the Tarot is here to help you learn about yourself, but this doesn't mean that it wants you to become self-centered.

If you worry too much, you may start to become quite self-centered or think that the world revolves around you and your problems. Every Tarot reading you do will always draw attention to other people so that you won't get wrapped up in your own worries and become oblivious to the needs of others. Always the emphasis is on helping yourself so that you, in turn, can help others.

Hopes and Dreams

You can be anything you want, but do be realistic and *work* toward what you want. A lot of teens say they want to be a movie star or a sports star, which means they wouldn't have to do any schoolwork. What they forget is that to succeed in these industries you have to work incredibly hard and make lots of personal sacrifices. We are not being killjoys here, but the odds of making it in the entertainment or sports world are very small. And even if you do make it, you will be eaten alive if you have not developed your brain. This is particularly true in the sports industry; after you turn thirty or so very few people want you, and you still have a lifetime ahead of you.

If you think you know what you want to do with your life, try this exercise. If you aren't sure, try the next exercise.

Fun Exercise, Part 1

Pick a card from the pack that signifies your chosen career, or something close to it. The following might help.

- The Magician: Sales and marketing
- The High Priestess: Psychic work, healing arts, alternative medicine
- The Empress: Midwife, nurse, doctor
- The Hierophant: Church work
- The Chariot: Sports

- Strength: Dentist
- Wheel of Fortune: Stockbroker
- Justice: Lawyer
- The World: Scientist
- Three of Cups: Entertainer
- Three of Wands: Travel industry
- Three of Pentacles: Artist, graphic designer
- Seven of Cups: Journalist, writer
- Eight of Pentacles: Builder, farmer, construction worker
- Nine of Cups: Chef, restaurant owner
- Ten of Pentacles: Homemaker
- Page of Wands: Librarian
- Knight of Swords: Technology
- Knight of Pentacles: Sales assistant
- Queen of Pentacles: Environment/gardening
- King of Cups: Teacher
- King of Pentacles: Business

If you can't find anything here, take a look at the Minor Arcana personality traits we listed in Part Two, and see if you can find a card in your chosen suit that best matches your aspirations.

When you have chosen your career card, shuffle the rest of the pack, thinking about what you need to do to achieve success in your career.

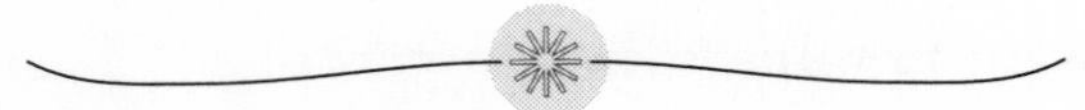

Don, sixteen, choose The Magician, because he would like to follow his father and work in sales and marketing. He then shuffled the pack and came up with the King of Pentacles and Six of Swords. This is telling him that his father, the King of Pentacles, is a good role model and guide for him. Pentacles is the card of the practical. It is telling him that the best way he can get ahead is just by doing. His father should be able to introduce him to some local companies who could use some help from a young person. However, in the long run he would need to broaden his experience in sales and marketing by traveling out of state to work for bigger international companies. The Six of Swords is the card of traveling. Great success is indicated in the long run.

Fun Exercise, Part 2

One of your biggest worries may be what you are going to do with the rest of your life. If this is the case, the cards will always advise that you put effort into your schoolwork so that you can have a broad range of career choices later in life. This exercise might be useful for those of you who are uncertain about future career choices.

If you don't know what you want to do in your career, pick three cards at random after having shuffled the pack, and use this book to work out their meanings.

Cynthia got the Four of Swords, the Queen of Cups, and The Lovers. The Four of Swords is telling Cynthia not to worry. As time goes on she will find out what she wants to do. There is no need for instant decisions. The Queen of Cups is suggesting that she will find happiness in jobs that involve communicating to others as well as helping them. The Lovers suggests that once she finds her niche in life, she will became quite passionate about it.

Whatever you do in life, remember that it is not what you do, it is how you do it. It is quite possible to be a happy garbage collector and an unhappy business tycoon.

Never Stop Hoping and Dreaming

Let the cards remind you that however hard life gets, however much it hurts when you get dumped, flunk your exams, or lose your friends, you still have hope. There is always hope that you will change, that things will improve, that you will find an answer to your problems. The future is never fixed. The cards show you that the outcome of your story is not a certainty, but a possibility. You can always change the situation if you have the desire and the courage to take the necessary steps.

If you feel that you keep making mistakes, so what? If you keep trying, keep learning from your setbacks, and remain optimistic, you will eventually get to where you want to go. Never forget that you have within you all you need to succeed. You won't be able to find it anywhere else. You are the beginning and the end. You have the power and the magic within you. Let the Tarot cards help you find that power and magic.

A Life of Discovery

The future is never fixed. The Tarot can highlight possible futures for you. It can advise, warn you of potential dangers, and encourage you to make better life choices, but it cannot make decisions for you. You and only you are the one who decides what is going to happen in your life.

Quick Fun Exercise

The way you approach problems in life will make or break you. Ask the Tarot the following question: "Do I handle problems and setbacks well?" Lay out seven cards. The first two cards you pick represent how you have been approaching problems; the next three cards represent how you are facing problems now; and the final two cards suggest the best way for you to handle problems in the future.

The Tarot can only hint at possible futures. A life in the cards is a life of discovery. It is a life of knowledge, excitement, wonder, and change. Ahead of you lie many exciting and wonderful things, as well as some strange and sad things. Sometimes you will get what you want, and sometimes you won't. Just remember that the secret of happiness doesn't lie in getting what you want; the true art of living is found in how you react to the changing situations you find yourself in. Let the Tarot help you react with wisdom, courage, and optimism. Let the Tarot help you treat triumph and disaster just the same. Let the Tarot help you keep your head when all around are losing theirs. Let the Tarot help you discover what an amazing human being you are.

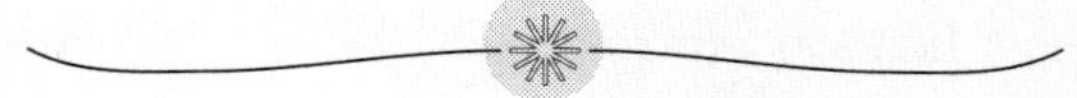

Final Fun Exercise

Do you remember the first exercise you did, way back in Chapter 6? You have been on quite a journey since then. Go back and find those five cards you chose, and place them in front of you. Think about what you have learned since then. Would you choose those five cards now? Now shuffle the rest of the pack and choose a card. Place this on top of the five cards, study the picture in detail, and think about what the card is trying to tell you.

We hope that this book will be the start of a lifelong friendship with the Tarot, and that in years to come you will revisit this book with fond memories. We hope, too, that it will one day remind you of a time of curiosity, wonder, enthusiasm, hope, and endless possibilities.

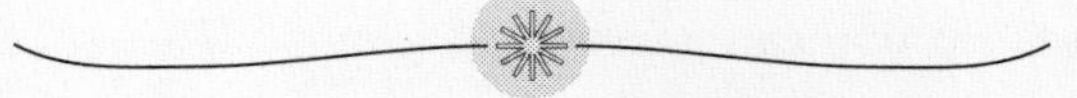

About the Authors

A brother-and-sister writing team, Theresa and Terry come from a family of psychics and have been interested in the Tarot since childhood.

Terry is currently working full-time as a psychic counselor and Tarot card reader. Prior to that he earned an M.A. from London University and worked for ten years as a secondary school drama teacher. He lives in South London with his partner.

Before writing full-time, Theresa earned an honors degree from King's College, Cambridge University, and a master's degree from King's College, London University. She has worked for a New Age publisher, taught English in secondary schools, been a freelance health consultant, and has read Tarot cards professionally for many years. The author of twelve self-help books, Theresa lives in Windsor, United Kingdom, with her husband and two young children.

To contact the authors:

If you wish to contact the authors, please write to them in care of Adams Media, and we will forward your request. Both the authors and the publisher appreciate hearing from you and learning how the book has helped you. Please write to:

Theresa Cheung and Terry Silvers
c/o Adams Media Corporation
57 Littlefield Street
Avon, MA 02322, U.S.A.

Please enclose a self-addressed envelope for reply.
Alternatively, you can e-mail us at *tcheung710@aol.com*.